FROM INSIGHT TO ACTION

Six New Ways to Think, Lead, and Achieve

Jean S. Frankel and Gabriel Eckert, CAE

★ **asae**
association
management
press

WASHINGTON, DC

The authors have worked diligently to ensure that all information in this book is accurate as of the time of publication and consistent with standards of good practice in the general management community. As research and practice advance, however, standards may change. For this reason it is recommended that readers evaluate the applicability of any recommendations in light of particular situations and changing standards.

ASAE: The Center for Association Leadership
Association Management Press
1575 I Street, NW
Washington, DC 20005-1103
Phone: (202) 626-2723; (888) 950-2723 outside the metropolitan Washington, DC
    area
Fax: (202) 220-6439
Email: books@asaecenter.org
We connect great ideas and great people to inspire leadership and achievement in the association community.

Keith C. Skillman, CAE, Vice President, Publications,
    ASAE: The Center for Association Leadership
Baron Williams, CAE, Director of Book Publishing,
    ASAE: The Center for Association Leadership
Cover and interior by Troy Scott Parker, Cimarron Design, cimarrondesign.com

This book is available at a special discount when ordered in bulk quantities. For information, contact the ASAE Member Service Center at (202) 371-0940.

A complete catalog of titles is available on the ASAE website at www.asaecenter.org.

ISBN-13: 978-0-88034-359-6
ISBN-10: 0-88034-359-1

Printed in the United States of America.

10 9 8 7 6 5 4 3 2

Contents

....

Foreword   vii

Preface   xi

Acknowledgements   xv

Introduction   xvii

   Drivers of a New Leadership Paradigm   xviii

      Uncontrollable Change   xviii

      The Dynamics of a Changing Workforce   xix

      The Future Flow of Work   xx

      Ideas Replacing Data   xx

      Technology and Social Media   xxii

      Big Data Versus Big Think   xxiii

   From Insight to Action: A New Leadership Paradigm   xxiv

   Emerging Competencies   xxv

   Essential Foundations   xxvii

PART I

Six Emerging Leadership Competencies

An Overview of Six Emerging Competencies   3

CHAPTER 1

360-Degree Thinking   7

      Interconnectedness   9

      Connessione and Systems Thinking   10

      Information Filters   12

      Whole-Brain Thinking   14

      How 360-Degree Thinking Would Have Helped One Professional Association   18

CHAPTER 2

Heightened Intuition 23

Defining *Intuition* 25
Characteristics of Intuition 27
Link to Emotional Intelligence 28
Leaders' Use of Intuition in Decision-Making 29
Shared Intuition 32
Case Study of Shared Intuition on an Association Board 36
Shared Intuition Is Not Groupthink 39
The Use of Intuition Does Not Come Without Controversy 43
What Leaders Can Do to Improve Their Capacity for Shared Intuition 45

CHAPTER 3

Dynamic Decision-Making 51

The Case for a New Way to Make Decisions 52
The Delicate Balance 53
A Dynamic Decision-Making Model 54
When It Makes Sense to Use Intuitive Decision-Making 58
Case Study of the Use of Dynamic Decision-Making 59

CHAPTER 4

Powerful Questions 63

Questions Create an Empowering Workplace 64
Powerful Questions in Facilitation 65
Understanding the Power of a Question 66
A Framework for Four Kinds of Powerful Questions 68
Asking Powerful Questions Requires Good Listening 71
Asking Powerful Questions Takes Courage 72
Asking Questions Enables Learning 73

CHAPTER 5

Diversity of Thought 77

The Dimensions of Diversity 79
Inborn Human Characteristics 80
Generational Diversity 81
Gender 83
Geographic and Cultural Diversity 83
Personal Experiences 86
Organizational Dimensions 87
Style and Tendencies 88
Board Composition and Diversity of Thought 92

CHAPTER 6
Understanding Change 95
Underlying Factors Affecting Change 96
Overcoming Immunity to Change 98
The Role of Coaching in Readying People for Change 99
The Role of Leadership 102

PART II
Eight Essential Organizational Foundations

CHAPTER 7
Eight Essential Organizational Foundations—An Overview 107
Purpose 112
Principles 114
Potential 118
Process 121
Priorities 125
People 127
Praise 130
Planet 131

PART III
One Unifying Strategy—Co-Creation

CHAPTER 8
Co-Creating the Future: How Leaders Lead Together 137
Three Levels of Co-Creation 138
A Continuum of Connection and Commitment 139
The Role of Leadership in Co-Creation 142
Co-Creation Breaks Down Organizational Silos 144
Co-Creation in Decision-Making 145
Case Study: Co-Creating the Future 145

CHAPTER 9
What Gets in the Way: Barriers to Success 153
Personality-Based Leadership 154
Pet Projects 154
Politics, Polarization, and Posturing 154
Protecting the Past 155

CHAPTER 10

Ideas for Action: How to Think, Lead, and Achieve in Your Organization   157

Adopt a More Holistic/Multidimensional Leadership View   157
Get Acquainted With Your Values and Intuition   158
Develop Dynamic Decision-Making Skills   159
Be More Connected to the People in the Organization   159
Ask Powerful Questions   160
Be More Conscious of the World Around You   160
Start the Conversation   161

Thoughts to Consider— An Individual and Organizational Diagnostic   163

Thoughts to Consider About the Six Emerging Leadership Competencies   164

Thoughts to Consider About the Eight Essential Foundations   166

Thoughts to Consider About the Unifying Strategy of Co-Creation: How Leaders Lead Together   171

Sources and Suggested Reading   173

Foreword

....

AMONG THE CHALLENGES THAT associations face today, none is more important than the building of leadership capacity. Without effective volunteer and staff leaders, associations are less able to successfully navigate the rocky and complex waters ahead. *From Insight to Action: Six New Ways to Think, Lead, and Achieve* provides an outstanding new take on competencies that leaders will need to move their organizations forward in the coming years.

Although my association has been successful for many years, one of the most personally satisfying elements of my role as CEO has been to develop individual leaders and watch their success over time. No less than four of our former staff are successful CEOs in their own right now, and many of our former volunteer leaders play important roles in leading healthcare into the future. Association leadership is about not only setting direction and achieving organizational success but also building individual capacity through mentorship and competency development.

Viewed through the lens of the individual staff or member leader, *From Insight to Action* identifies six new ways of thinking that help to enhance dialogue, encourage critical thinking, and embrace diversity of thought as well as eight essential organizational foundations necessary to support new ways of thinking and leading. The authors make the point that associations in recent years have been particularly focused on data—"metrics, mechanisms, and minutiae"—and that a focus on data alone does not guarantee good decisions or effective leadership. Rather, Frankel and Eckert advocate here for the addition of intuition, insight, and ideas into the leadership mix.

In the first section, the authors suggest six emerging new focus areas for individual leaders to engage and develop competency in:

- Practicing 360-degree thinking, being cognizant of ideas and insights coming from a variety of sources, both internally and externally, and understanding the critical interconnectedness of these ideas;

- Developing a heightened sense of internal intuition, which the authors define as the art of blending knowledge with internal or shared perception to make better decisions;

- Using dynamic decision-making, a framework for determining whether a decision should be made more on intuition or data;

- Increasing the use of powerful questions, which help not only to gather data and insights but also to recognize patterns and make meaning;

- Achieving diversity of thought by seeing, valuing, and embracing differences of thinking styles, personal experiences, style tendencies, and inborn human characteristics, not just demographics; and

- Understanding the true nature of change, which illuminates the factors underlying people's ability to absorb and embrace change.

All these competencies have implications for individual leaders and their ability to reason and make effective decisions, as well as for associations and organizations, where leaders are able to practice and model these competencies and move forward with relevance into the future.

The second section details eight essential organizational foundations that the authors deem necessary to have in place, including sufficient understanding of the organization's purpose, articulation of principles and values, a clear statement of vision or potential, effective processes for work and decision-making, methodologies for selecting priorities, understanding of the role the organization plays in its external community, and mechanisms for developing people and praising their efforts. *From Insight to Action: Six New Ways to Think, Lead, and Achieve* encourages leaders and their organizations to be more aware of ideas, patterns, intercon- nections, and implications. It helps association leaders to more effectively "connect the dots" in this time when there are more choices, more challenges, and more uncertainty than ever before.

The authors present these concepts not as a cookbook of what to do but rather as a portrait of "how to be" as a leader. It is an excellent basis for mentorship, thought leadership, and effective capacity building. *From Insight to Action: Six New Ways to Think, Lead, and Achieve* is incisive, thought-provoking, and an essential read for all who lead associations now and for all who aspire to do so in the future.

   – Thomas C. Dolan, PhD, FACHE, CAE
     President and Chief Executive Officer
     American College of Healthcare Executives

Preface

OVER THE PAST FEW years, the association community has been the target of many books about structures and mechanisms—how to change the governance system, how to change committee structures, how to change the nominations process, how to do strategic planning, and more.

This book is a response to all the advice that association leaders have been given about restructuring, reorganizing, measuring, monitoring, and quantifying the performance of their organizations, with a suggestion that perhaps they should increase their focus on something else, namely, leadership.

Many books have been written about leadership competencies and leading organizational change efforts, but most of them are focused on the corporate sector and few can be applied to associations. Leading an association is different from leading in the for-profit sector, and this book is designed to provide association leaders and future association leaders with an understanding of the skills they need to enhance or acquire to ensure their success as association leaders and the success of their associations.

Great businesses are associated with long-term leaders. Steve Jobs at Apple, Jack Welch at GE, and Warren Buffett are examples of successful long-term business leaders. In association management, we cannot rely on the singular and continual influence of long-term leaders to delegate, empower, and inspire. Rather, leadership in associations is shared among volunteers who rotate through positions of influence and staff who provide an important component of continuity and organizational memory.

Over the last few years, association leaders have become so focused on the infrastructure of boards, staffs, committees, member engagement, social media, and all the other mechanisms necessary for successful associations, that they have lost sight of the broader concepts of leadership. Perhaps association leaders have been too focused on metrics, mechanics, and minutia. In many cases, all the things leaders have been told to do have failed to move the needle toward organizational long-term goals, visions, and aspirations.

In the quest to get the systems, structures, and processes right, is it possible that association leaders have not allowed themselves sufficient time to focus on their roles and competencies as leaders?

It is time for association leaders (and future leaders) to step back and see the larger picture of what they are doing and how it all fits together. It is time to regain sight of the importance of leadership competency and the roles that individual leaders play in making good things happen.

This book encourages a more holistic approach for association leadership than is common today. It highlights six emerging and important individual leadership competencies and reminds us of eight essential organizational foundations that must be in place before even the best leader can be successful. We hear association leaders asking themselves, "What will it take to lead successfully in our increasingly complex environments? What will leaders need to do to help their organizations achieve full potential and sustain positive change? What will enable leaders to engage, lead, and thrive in the future?"

We created this book to answer those questions.

From Insight to Action details six emerging competencies that leaders will need in the increasingly amorphous and complex organizational ecosystems in which they will function, eight essential organizational foundations that will need to be in place (and we hope they already are to some extent) in all organizations, and one unifying strategy—co-creation. Through these chapters, readers will gain insight into these ideas, and will take away high-level leadership strategies for effecting and sustaining change in an increasingly fluid environment.

Although *From Insight to Action* will provide guidelines and suggestions for developing these competencies, this book does not tell you precisely what to do; rather, it suggests how to be as a leader; how to execute your leadership role; what kinds of things to focus on in your organizational environment, in your member environment, in your professional community, and in the world in which you live.

It doesn't tell you what to think, but rather what you might begin to think about and, more importantly, how you will need to think to embrace a broader and more complex association environment.

Unlike other recent association leadership books, the bulk of the content of this book is focused through the lens of the leader—the CEO; the board chair or board member; or staff executive, director, or manager—rather than through the lens of the organization. We devote much of the text to the individual leader's role and competencies—the what and how of leadership in an ever-evolving environment. Although focused on member and staff leaders at the executive level, we hope that anyone at any level in an association who has the passion to continually grow and learn will find value in this book.

And although the book's message is directed most specifically to association leaders, its content is derived from consultation with leaders from many sectors—governmental organizations, for-profit corporations, nonprofit philanthropic foundations and cause-related organizations, trade associations, and professional societies. In our interviews, we found overwhelming support for our ideas from leaders across all these sectors, and so we hope that leaders in many kinds of organizations will find our thinking to be of value both individually and for their organizations.

Acknowledgements

···

THIS BOOK IS THE work of a team of consultant and practitioner. Jean Frankel has more than 18 years of association consulting experience, and more than 30 years of business management consulting experience across all major sectors. Gabriel Eckert is a working chief staff officer with more than 10 years of experience in the nonprofit sector and involvement in local and national organizations. This pairing of consultant and practitioner provides a unique perspective on the issues, challenges, and solutions provided in this book.

We would like to extend a special thanks to the Ideas for Action, LLC, research team of Vinay Kumar; Nancy Alexander, MBA; and Jay McNaught, MBA, PhD; as well as colleagues and collaborators Chris Oronzi; John Krister Lowe; Elizabeth M. Lucas, CAE, MBA; Carrie Mattingly; Christopher W. Seiz; Mychelle Blake; Jim Moody, CAE; Wendy Kavanagh, CAE; Cheryl Ronk, CAE; C. Diane Matt, CAE; Sherrie Cade; and Judy Gray, CAE.

In our research for this book, we have drawn upon our collective knowledge of working with hundreds of organizations in the trade, professional, and philanthropic sectors of the not-for-profit world as well as the corporate world, academia, government, and non-governmental organizations. We thank the many leaders interviewed for this book, for their courage, collaboration, and candor.

We also owe a debt of gratitude to two outstanding university executive education programs: Columbia University Teacher's

College and Columbia Business School's Executive and
Organizational Coaching Program and the Coles College of Business
Executive MBA Program at Kennesaw State University. Frankel has
engaged in recent study at Columbia and Eckert at Kennesaw State,
and the knowledge gained through their studies has fundamentally
reshaped their views of leadership.

Jean Frankel would especially like to thank Columbia University
Coaching Certification Program faculty members Rachel Ciporen,
PhD;. Terrence Maltbia, PhD; and David Matthew Prior, MBA,
MCC; as well as her fellow Cohort VII coaches and C3P alumni,
an amazing global learning community that has inspired new
exploration into thought leadership.

Gabriel Eckert would especially like to thank Alison Keefe,
PhD; Chris Rumsey; Stephen Brock, PhD; Paul Lopez, PhD; Alvin
Miles, PhD; Steve Smalt, PhD; Michael Salvador, PhD; and the
entire faculty of the Executive MBA Program at the Coles College
of Business at Kennesaw State University as well as the cohort
of 2011. The curriculum of the program creates leaders with an
expanded understanding of global business, executive coaching, and
leadership.

Eckert would also like to express deep appreciation to the
members, leaders, and staff of the Building Owners and Managers
Association of Georgia. BOMA Georgia has proven that members
and staff can truly achieve and maintain positive change, effectively
serve an industry, and co-create the future. Additionally, the entire
BOMA International federation, including members and staff, has
contributed greatly to the author's understanding of association
governance and success.

We would also like to thank Keith Skillman, CAE; Baron Williams,
CAE; and the ASAE publishing team for their support, vision, and
guidance throughout this project.

Lastly, Frankel would like to thank her husband, Barry J. Frankel,
for his unwavering faith, support, patience, and love.

  – Jean Frankel
    Gabriel Eckert
    July 2012

Introduction

T HERE HAS NEVER BEEN a more complex time to be a leader. More information, more decisions, and more activity are universally expected outcomes. Experts say that the growth of data has now reached an unsustainable level. In the coming years, association leaders increasingly will find themselves deep inside a sort of "information vortex," with infinite ideas for programs, services, and strategies swirling around them and with little control over the origin or destination of these ideas.

What will it take for association leaders to succeed in this new, more complex information vortex? What competencies will be required to manage ideas, rather than system structures, processes, and data? What will leaders and organizations need to do well?

We believe that the challenge for leaders and organizations will be to cope with and navigate through an ever-increasing data flow, resulting in the need for the next paradigm of leadership. *From Insight to Action: Six New Ways to Think, Lead, and Achieve* presents a framework for emerging leadership competencies and essential organizational foundations. It is what leaders will need to master to go from managing data to managing ideas and to succeed in a constantly changing environment.

Drivers of a New Leadership Paradigm

Uncontrollable Change

Change is increasing in speed. And in this increasing speed of change, one of the biggest challenges for leaders will be to make effective decisions to navigate their organizations through complex times. In their book *Geeks and Geezers* (2002), Bennis and Thomas compare senior leaders to emerging young leaders. The authors point out that for leaders to remain viable, they must continue learning because the world is changing at a tremendous pace. "The world has changed more in the eighty or so years since our oldest leaders were born than it had in the previous millennium." Although this research focuses on corporate sector organizations, it has equal relevance to associations.

The pace of change has not slowed and is not likely to do so in our lifetimes. Association leaders will need to be more flexible, more fluid, and more multidimensional in their approach. Strategies that are working now will need to be rethought, even before they have had a chance to be completed. Association leaders will need to both sort out in their own minds and help those they lead to understand, accept, and embrace change.

Leaders can no longer implement change and merely look straight ahead. They must develop the capability to look at all sides of issues and all levels of timing. Leaders who are unable to absorb all that is happening around them at any given time will be left behind. This environment will require that association leaders possess not only advanced thinking skills but also the ability to develop enough self-awareness and understanding to be able to move past their own internal barriers to change.

Competition within and outside the association sector is increasing, and the role of associations is quickly evolving. How do leaders manage change in an unmanageable world? Smart leaders have discovered that control is an illusion at best. Can anyone really "manage" change—in people or in organizations? What will be needed to lead in this environment? How will leaders create and sustain positive change in what will undoubtedly be an even more complex future? What foundations will need to exist within organizations, and what competencies will leaders need to possess to achieve and sustain positive change amidst increasing complexity? What will it actually look and feel like when change is sustained over time in the future?

In the face of these challenges, as well as the recent economic pressures that have in some cases significantly affected the typical association's capacity and forward momentum, association leaders have been trying to regain control in an increasingly out-of-control environment. Leaders have been trying to control the uncontrollable through new models for governance, work, decision-making systems, and strategic planning. Most of these models attempt to manage data in its many forms or create mechanisms to create, process, and act upon data.

The Dynamics of a Changing Workforce

The dynamics of a changing workforce are among the drivers of new association leader competencies. Obviously, the overall demographics of the workforce are changing. Among the demographic trends that are of particular interest is that a growing number of baby boomers are remaining in the workforce.

The presence of older workers implies that many leaders in organizations are also aging, and this is true in the volunteer workforce of associations as well. In an increasingly complex environment, when the quantity of data is increasing and the role of intuition in decision-making will increase, organizations with experienced, mature leaders may be at increased risk of faulty decisions if leaders have not developed the competencies of intuition and dynamic decision-making to make effective decisions using these approaches.

Despite generational demographics, workforces are becoming less responsive to command-and-control leadership styles, and although the work and decision-making structures in associations are different, the workforce may still be subject to hierarchical, control-oriented leadership. In our emerging new world, followers want leaders who will empower them and not control them. In *The Leadership Challenge* (2007), Kouzes and Pozner offer practical advice, "In a productive work community, leaders are not commanders and controllers, bosses and big shots. They are servers and supporters, partners and providers. In this new world, competencies such as seeking diversity of thought, asking powerful questions, and understanding the nature of change are essential."

The Future Flow of Work

In the future, the flow of work will no longer happen in a logical, rational, serial order. Ideas will be coming faster and from a more complex variety of sources. In this crush of information, models, and pronouncements, there will be little time for contemplation, for looking at the big picture, for stepping back and seeing how the pieces fit. It will be a challenge for association leaders to make the time and have the vision to see the interconnectedness of things, to see how one idea can build on another and how one decision affects another.

Ideas Replacing Data

Ideas are quickly replacing data as the organizational assets of value, and ideas that can be acted on are even more essential. As Hindu Prince Gautama Siddhartha (563–483 B.C.), the founder of Buddhism, stated, "An idea that is developed and put into action is more important than an idea that exists only as an idea." How will association leaders move from managing the flow of data to leading the development of ideas?

And in terms of managing ideas, what is actually known about the nature of an idea anyway? Is any idea actually, truly original? Can ideas exist in a vacuum? Can any idea exist that has not in some way been built on a previous one? The answer is almost undoubtedly no. Examine any idea more closely, and it will become apparent that it has foundations in an earlier idea or ideas, likely built on and supported by even more ideas. In other words, ideas are interrelated.

In identifying, articulating, and evaluating concepts, thinking often goes from one idea to another in no logical or serial form. Ideas need each other's support for their expression. In fact, they are so dependent on each other that, more often than not, idea A cannot even be conceived without conceiving of ideas B, C, and D. Ideas are like living organisms; they take shape from other ideas, evolve with other ideas, and are eventually replaced by newer ones.

In many ways, ideas actually form an ecosystem, and association leaders will be functioning within an ecosystem (or ecosystems) of ideas. The ecosystem of ideas may not exist solely inside an association but also within a membership base, an industry, a community, or the world at large.

Ecosystems in nature are complex communities in which living things interact with both living and nonliving elements within their environment. Ecosystems vary greatly in size, but one thing is always the same: Every element in an ecosystem is dependent on the other elements. If one part of an ecosystem is damaged or disappears, everything else is affected. Central to the ecosystem concept is the idea that all elements of an ecosystem are linked together through a nutrient cycle, or flow of energy. Living organisms interact with every other element in their local environment, so a flow of positive energy is created.

James F. Moore (*The Death of Competition: Leadership and Strategy in the Age of Business Ecosystems,* 1997) links this concept to business ecosystems, and here we can link it to the idea of associations functioning as ecosystems.

What elements are interconnected in your association's ecosystem of ideas? From where does your idea energy flow? Where and how will new ideas emerge? Will the process be cyclical? Predictable? Serial? In what form will ideas surface? Will they be in 30-page committee white papers or 140-character tweets? Will they come from an association's established volunteers, or will they emerge unexpectedly from others, those who haven't been involved previously but for some reason, spontaneously choose to engage at any given time?

In the future, there will be a need for leaders who can think and absorb multiple ideas, on multiple levels, from multiple sources, in multiple time frames, and in multiple ways. Leaders will need the ability to balance, judge, and access all available brain power to navigate in this new ecosystem of ideas. Leaders will need to be multidimensional thinkers. They will need to harness their

An Organizational Ecosystem

FIGURE 1. *Ecosystem of Emerging Competencies and Essential Organizational Foundations*

right-brain aesthetic, feeling, creative side as well as their left-brain, rational, logical, analytical side.

There will be a significant demand for leaders who are more holistic, multidimensional thinkers. Leaders will need to have the ability to filter and balance what is heard with what is felt or believed to make the best decisions. The inevitable information overload will require leaders to learn to swim in richer, deeper, and more complex and crowded waters—to live and function within an ecosystem of ideas.

Technology and Social Media

Another driver of the need for new leadership competencies is that social media and advanced technology have dramatically changed how we communicate, interact, think, and make decisions.

Everything is interconnected. Personal opinions mix with professional priorities. Family and friends might coexistent in a virtual conversation with clients and colleagues. What is put on Facebook can instantaneously and automatically be posted on Twitter, LinkedIn, Pinterest, and other social media platforms. A single poorly worded personal opinion, posted on Facebook, may affect a relationship with a member or client.

The evolution of social media and technology means that simple linear thinking is no longer sufficient. Conversations and information flow are much more complex and will be even more so in the future, in an environment where individuals multitask, leveraging multiple social media platforms and mobile electronic devices simultaneously. How we communicate in a world of technology must be mirrored by how we think.

In a world where organizations have often functioned in silos, there are now fewer silos. The personal and organizational walls have been stripped down. In this environment, association leaders will need to be more comfortable working in a broader, more open environment. This means it will be impossible to make a change in one part of an organization without affecting another.

Big Data Versus Big Think

We have become inundated with data as a result of this technology-charged environment. Metrics, mechanics, and minutia have become key focuses in many organizations, and in some cases may have been given too high a priority.

But data alone can never solve a problem and cannot solely predict the future. Data alone will not lead to the right choices and alone cannot be a sustainable basis for decision-making.

In a *Harvard Business Review* article in April of 2012, "Good Data Won't Guarantee Good Decisions," Shah, Horne, and Capellá make the point that many organizations have made large investments in information technology and in people management in what's referred to as "big data." They note, "For all the breathless promises about the return on investment in big data, companies face a challenge. Investments in analytics can be useless, even harmful, unless employees can incorporate that data into complex decision-making."

Leaders must learn to balance this "big data" with big thinking—their own intuition, insight, and perspectives—and must become competent in engaging groups in their organizations to do the same. We believe that the time is right for a greater emphasis on intuition and the need for a more balanced method of decision-making that does not emphasize knowledge alone but acknowledges and respects the need for a true balance between what is known in a leader's head and what is felt in a leader's gut.

Many associations have practiced data-driven decision-making for years and have developed competency in collecting, cataloging, and evaluating data and then summarizing it for use by boards of directors, committees, and other work groups.

However, this has not always led organizations to make good decisions. And for many associations, it has not enabled them to sustain organizational change. Association leadership will require competencies embracing a heightened sense of individual intuition and the ability to integrate that intuition into organizational decision-making processes that are more dynamic.

From Insight to Action: A New Leadership Paradigm

So we must ask: In the crush of data and decision-making; in the cloud of mechanics, metrics, and minutia; under the mounds of advice about how to structure our organizations, how to measure progress, and how to reorganize the data; and in the relative aftermath of an economy that has put significant pressures on associations to merely survive, have association leaders lost focus on who they are as leaders and as people? Have association leaders somehow minimized their focus on understanding, nurturing, and maximizing the human capital that makes up an organization? Are the leadership competencies of today enough to take us through to an uncertain tomorrow?

Emerging Competencies

The leadership competencies of the past are no longer sufficient. Leaders must learn new ways to think, lead, and achieve. What competencies will association leaders need? What will these leaders do? How will they behave? How will they think, and what will they think about? In this book, we present six emerging ways to think, lead, and achieve. Here are some questions to consider:

- Do your association's leaders understand the fundamental interconnectedness of ideas?

- Do they see how that understanding leads to more multidimensional thinking, which leads to better decisions?

- Do they understand that decision-making, now more than ever, needs to be a thoughtful blend of the data-driven methodologies that we have been taught to employ with the innate intuition that we all possess? How many of your leaders understand and are comfortable using a system of dynamic decision-making where there is a balance between quantitative data and qualitative instincts, blending the recognition of patterns, the foresight of perceptions, the feel of what's right? Are your leaders empowered and enabled to make the right decision at the right time for the right reasons?

- Do your leaders have an effective connection with their own intuition? Do your leaders understand that intuition is a unique combination of brain function, values, emotions, and gut feel? Do your leaders fully understand the power of using intuition in their decision-making? Have your leaders heightened their awareness of their own intuition enough to be able to understand their internal compass must be balanced in any decision with quantitative data?

- Do your boards engage in diversity of thought? Diversity is not a new concept for associations. However, while many boards of directors have sufficient diversity based on traditional demographic variables, has that resulted in sufficient diversity in their thinking? Is your board composed of not just a mix of geographic, demographic, and ethnographic variables that represent your profession but also a balance of right-brain and left-brain thinkers and people who think big picture as well as those who are detail oriented? Do you have a combination of those who see the world from the past and those who are focused on the future?

• Do your leaders understand the power of a question? Do they understand that to help an association achieve and sustain its full potential sometimes the question is more powerful than the answer? Do they understand the importance of and, in fact, use open-ended, explorative, engaging questions to develop creative, collaborative, and sometimes courageous conversations? What questions are your leaders afraid to ask each other and themselves? What new leadership competencies will be needed to bring those questions to the surface?

• To what extent do your association's leaders understand that good questioning also includes good listening? Do they understand that listening happens on a variety of levels and that deep listening involves understanding what others are saying and what they really mean?

• Do your association's leaders understand the underlying drivers of change? When communicating vision and proposing change, do they understand the impact on people in terms of their hopes, assumptions, and fears? Do they understand the barriers to change that exist in individuals and how to help themselves and others move past those obstacles?

• Are your leaders skilled at using emerging competencies to co-create the future? Do they know how to build relationships in a way that maximizes the full capacity of human capital both inside and outside your association, with both staff and volunteers?

• Finally, are you as a leader creating an organizational environment where all of these questions can be asked, where these competencies can be used, where a culture of collaboration helps ensure that each individual participates in a meaningful way, both personally and professionally?

Essential Foundations

In addition to learning new competencies, association leaders must also ensure that their organization's foundational systems, structures, and processes are healthy. We see the emerging competencies and the organizational foundations coexisting in a sort of organizational ecosystem.

When an ecosystem is healthy, scientists say it is sustainable, meaning all the elements are in balance. A necessary question then becomes, "Is your association's organizational ecosystem balanced?"

Certain organizational foundations are necessary for an association to have a balanced ecosystem: purpose, principles, potential, process, priorities, people, praise, and planet. These foundations are explored in detail in Chapter 9. Successful leaders must ask themselves which organizational foundations are functioning most effectively within their organization and which need improvement or greater focus. The most successful leaders will also ask how these foundations are interrelated within their organization. Which organizational foundations are getting the greatest share of the attention of leaders? Which organizational foundations create the most energy for the organization? And finally, which of these is used in the organization in the most meaningful way to create positive change?

From Insight to Action is about the ability to balance, manage, understand, and leverage ideas. Multidimensional thinking will be required in the future because the questions leaders must address will be more difficult and the solutions will be less obvious. For all of its specific methodology, the data-driven culture has not become a panacea for all of the ills that plague associations and likely never will. Faced with this prospect, association leaders must learn new competencies to facilitate individual and organizational success.

In presenting these competencies and foundations in a framework that will benefit both individual leaders and their organizations, this book is divided into three parts:

The first part of the book introduces six emerging competencies: 360-degree thinking, heightened intuition, dynamic decision-making, powerful questions, diversity of thought, and understanding change.

The second part of the book explores the eight essential organizational foundations, which we regard as critical systems, structures, and processes that all associations should have in place to achieve and sustain positive change. They are the basic systems and processes that make for good association leadership. Much staff and volunteer leader attention has been focused on these essential elements, and many associations have achieved great success as a result. The focus of this part of the book is not only to briefly describe best practices in this area but also for association leaders to use the questions at the end of each description as an assessment to determine the relative strength of their organization in these basic competency areas. And we would add that it is not enough to merely have all of these in place. Successful association leaders can simultaneously monitor and understand the interactions among the competencies.

The third part of the book focuses on one unifying strategy: co-creation. Co-creation happens when members and staff are equally invested in not only the outcome but the process, not only the destination but the journey. How do they use the emerging leadership competencies and essential organizational foundations to lead sustained change together? The end of each chapter lists thoughts to consider in the form of questions. Although the book focuses more on the *what* than the *how*, this section will address ways in which leaders on all levels can think about and implement the concepts in this book. It addresses the question of how both individual leaders and leadership teams can institutionalize these leadership competencies and organizational foundations.

In some ways, this book raises more questions than it provides answers. That is its goal. We hope these questions will provoke rich, deep, and essential dialogues among leaders, members, and other stakeholders. We hope that leaders will learn and grow together. And we hope that the dialogues encouraged by this book will enable both leaders and organizations to work together more effectively to move from insight to action in ways that are unique to their own organization's culture.

There is no one right path to embracing and using the concepts in *From Insight to Action.* There is no cookbook solution. Association leaders must be prepared to see their organizations, and themselves, through new lenses and must begin to view their world in a new way. And we hope that this book will help readers move forward successfully in that journey.

PART I

Six Emerging Leadership Competencies

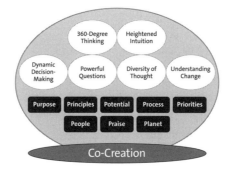

An Overview of Six Emerging Competencies

THE COMPLEXITY OF MANAGING ideas will require that associations and their leaders begin to think in new ways. The six emerging competencies that we have identified are all about viewing the world more holistically and multidimensionally. Decisions will not be simple; problems will not be straightforward; and dialogue and enfranchisement will become essential to an association's ability to achieve its full potential. Decisions will need to be made at the right time, in the right way, and for the right reasons.

In the following chapters we will consider six emerging competencies that will help leaders and their organizations move from insight to action.

- **360-Degree Thinking.** Understanding the fundamental interconnections of systems, structures, processes, culture, and ideas. Understanding the impact that changes in one have on another. Leadership ability to view ideas and information coming from all sides on all levels in all timeframes (for example, short-, medium-, and long-term priorities). The ability to absorb input on all levels at all times.

- **Heightened Intuition.** A holistic decision-making approach that considers and integrates information from all the senses. Individual leader skills that increase awareness of values, beliefs, and observations; recognize patterns in previous experiences; and rapidly process information, physically and mentally, to make effective decisions.

- **Dynamic Decision-Making.** A new model for determining to what extent data and intuition should be used when making decisions individually or in groups.

- **Powerful Questions.** Asking open-ended, reflective, courageous questions to which the leader does not seek a predetermined answer or outcome and actively listening and using follow-up questions to fully understand, facilitate, and illuminate both individual and group responses.

- **Diversity of Thought.** Creating work and leadership teams that include individuals with diverse experiences, cultures, and thinking preferences and having sufficient understanding of those differences to commit to the development of decision-making cultures that fully use the ideas and input of all, not just those who voice common ideas.

- **Understanding Change.** Understanding how the underlying mind-sets regarding change in individuals along with the collective mind-sets in organizations combine to create barriers to change. Understanding hidden fears and assumptions to unlock the ability for individuals and organizations to embrace change.

Among these competencies there are interconnections and themes, and a number of trends in leadership thinking have influenced our identification and selection of these competencies.

One theme that runs through a number of the competencies is the concept of whole-brain thinking. We are all familiar with right-brain and left-brain thinking. Left-brain thinking has become associated with command-and-control leadership, a style that is seen as less successful in the workplace. Some researchers argue that the complexity of today's organizations necessitate the use of more "right-brain" qualities such as conceptual thinking and intuition. In Chapter 1, we will explore the concept in the context of the emerging competency of 360-degree thinking, but we think it has significance for many of the other competencies as well.

Another theme that runs through many of the competencies is the concept that data-driven decision-making alone will not be sufficient for leaders and associations to navigate a challenging complex future. Associations have long been encouraged to practice data-driven decision-making. We believe that a new model of dynamic decision-making, in which leaders balance data with intuition, will become more important in the future, as complex decision-making will require leaders to rely more on values and values constructs than on data alone. Chapters 2 and 3 address the concepts of intuition and dynamic decision-making.

There is evidence of the need for these competencies in a variety of business sectors. Researchers report a growing acceptance of intuitive decision-making as a valid decision-making process. According to M. H. Bazerman (*Judgment in Managerial Decision-Making,* 2006), time and cost constraints limit the quantity and quality of available information. Bazerman adds that decision makers retain only a relatively small amount of information in their usable memory. He concludes that limitations on intelligence and perceptions constrain the ability of decision makers to accurately "calculate" the optimal choice from the information that is available. Bazerman surmises that together, these limitations prevent decision makers from making the optimal decisions assumed by the rational model.

Another general theme throughout is the need for association leaders to build competency in emotional intelligence. Originated by Daniel Goleman in his book *Emotional Intelligence: Why It Can Matter More Than IQ* (1997), the concept of emotional intelligence is all about leaders' gaining a greater understanding of their internal motivations and feelings and then translating that ability to be able to see more deeply into the beliefs, values, assumptions, motivators, and emotions of others. We cover emotional intelligence briefly in Chapter 2 in the context of building a heightened sense of intuition, but we encourage all association leaders to pursue further reading and study on this concept, as we believe it will be a huge component in the complex workplaces of tomorrow.

Each chapter concludes with a set of thoughts to consider. Some of these are intended for individual leaders, and others are meant to stimulate dialogue and conversation among boards, staff teams, and other workgroups. The competencies are complex but essential. These ideas are on the cusp of awareness among many progressive association leaders. We hope to raise awareness of and attention to these ideas so that others may use them to create emerging change and success in their organizations.

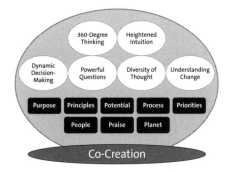

360-Degree Thinking | Heightened Intuition

Dynamic Decision-Making | Powerful Questions | Diversity of Thought | Understanding Change

Purpose | Principles | Potential | Process | Priorities

People | Praise | Planet

Co-Creation

CHAPTER 1

360-Degree Thinking

T HE FIRST OF THE emerging ways to think, lead, and achieve is 360-degree thinking. This emerging leadership competency requires leaders to look all around, and not just straight ahead. It suggests that leaders need to constantly see in three dimensions: the past, present, and future.

We define 360-degree thinking as an understanding of the fundamental interconnections of systems, structures, processes, culture, and ideas in multiple time and space modes. It's about understanding the impact that changes in one area have on another. It's about developing the capacity to view ideas and information coming from all sides on all levels and in all timeframes (for example, short-, medium-, and long-term priorities). And it is about the ability to absorb input on all levels at all times.

The concept of 360-degree thinking has dimensions of both time and space. It is related to time in that leaders need to look ahead to see future trends and goals, behind to see the past trends and clearly understand the organization's purpose and values, and to the side, seeing in the present with peripheral vision.

Leaders who look solely at the present can cause problems for their organizations. Far too often, leaders tend to look at data that is readily at hand. They look "straight ahead," consulting standard data sources and making decisions by paying the most attention to what is typically known and seen. There is a tendency for leaders to focus on the task at hand and on issues that are easily seen on the horizon, especially in an environment that demands more and more decisions at a faster and faster pace. Unfortunately, in doing so, association leaders often fail to see the larger picture, including information that may seem only tangentially relevant at the time of the decision but that will have long-term implications. The loss of peripheral vision results in tunnel vision, and this can be the result for association leaders who fail to use a 360-degree view of their environment.

Starting a new education business line? Your association may be significantly underestimating the competition in the marketplace, and there may be data available about activity in a tangential industry that is about to affect your members.

Distributing an official association e-newsletter on a bimonthly basis? Unfortunately, the real conversation about your association's agenda already may be happening on a member's Facebook page, a place that your association cannot control and may not even be able to monitor.

Making a change to your governance or board structure? There may be an important stakeholder group within your association that will feel disenfranchised by the change.

There is a growing need for association leaders to think on a broader level, adopt a deeper awareness, take the time to examine patterns and interconnections, and reflect on the deeper meaning of an issue or topic. The challenges required of association leaders in the future suggest that it is no longer sufficient to look straight ahead. Leaders must look all around themselves, all the time. Everything is interconnected, and decisions made in one part of an organization, or information applicable to one issue, may affect others. Look straight ahead at your own peril; look all around at all times, and you'll be moving toward 360-degree thinking.

Interconnectedness

One of the most significant aspects of 360-degree thinking is the concept of interconnectedness. This refers not just to the interconnection of information and ideas that can be gained through a 360-degree external view but also to organizational foundations that exist within every association: purpose, principles, potential, priorities, processes, people, and praise. (These will be explored in detail in Chapter 9.)

The concept of interconnectedness can be seen in the world around us. Just as a wide variety of elements in nature are essential for life and it is their interconnectedness that is key, so it is with this competency of leadership. In nature, the right balance within an ecosystem is necessary for life to flourish, and 360-degree thinking encourages a belief that ideas, actions, and information are interconnected throughout an organization.

We live in a world that is becoming increasingly interconnected. Social media creates an interconnectedness that didn't exist just a decade ago. As the world becomes more connected, leaders need to consider the organizational foundations within their own organizations and how they interrelate.

Association leaders need to understand the holistic nature of their organizations and the basic components of which they are composed. It is the interconnectedness of these organizational elements that is key. Just as the right balance within an ecosystem is necessary for life to flourish in nature, so within the organizational ecosystem, balance is an important characteristic of how the elements interact.

If we envision organizations as ecosystems, it is not simply the presence of these elements within organizations that enable them to be successful; it is their interconnectedness. Leaders who practice 360-degree thinking can capitalize on ideas and information that best support the association's purpose and principles; set priorities that are supported by operationally efficient processes; leverage the unique skills, knowledge, and talents of the association's people (both volunteers and staff) while genuinely expressing praise for their contributions; and as a result, turn ideas into reality and positively affect the world around them.

While each of the organizational foundations exists separately, their effectiveness is enhanced by considering the relationships among them. For example, in successful organizations, the interconnectedness of purpose and principles will drive the selection of priorities.

Connessione and Systems Thinking

As new as social media as a driver for 360-degree thinking is, the concept actually has its roots in the distant past. For more than five centuries, Western civilization has viewed with admiration and awe the life and works of Leonardo da Vinci, and believe it or not, 360-degree thinking is related to one of his great ideas.

Of the many roles that da Vinci played—astronomer, musician, scientist, inventor, and philosopher—part of his genius was that he actually recorded the methods he used in achieving that brilliance: how to think, how to develop and use our inherent capabilities, how to integrate everything we learn into one harmonious whole. And now, many centuries later, da Vinci's ideas have actually re-emerged in more contemporary management concepts such as "whole-brain thinking," "mind-body connection," "brainstorming," and "systems thinking."

One idea in particular relates specifically to our notion of 360-degree thinking and interconnectedness. In his book, *How to Think Like Leonardo da Vinci: Seven Steps to Genius Every Day* (1998), Michael Gelb identifies seven competencies that da Vinci originally articulated that helped him to think broadly and creatively. One is the concept called *connessione,* which means "recognizing and appreciating the interconnectedness of all things." Gelb notes, "When you toss a stone into a still pond, the water ripples out in a series of widening circles. Conjure up that image in your mind's eye: Ask yourself how one ripple affects another and where the energy of the ripples goes, and you will be thinking like da Vinci. The ever-expanding circle is an apt metaphor for the principle of *connessione,* which is evident in da Vinci's frequent observations of patterns and connections in the world around him."

To help us think in *connessione* terms, consider: If a butterfly flaps its wings in Tokyo, does it affect the weather in New York?

Contemporary systems theorists are fond of answering this classic question with an enthusiastic yes. Five centuries ago, da Vinci, the original systems thinker, noted that the earth is moved from its position by the weight of a tiny bird resting upon it.

As you are trying to use 360-degree thinking, trying to absorb all you see (and all that you don't), is it important to have it all organized? Over the years, scholars criticized da Vinci for the disorder of his notebooks. He never provided a table of contents, an outline, or an index. He scrawled notes in apparently random fashion, switched from topic to topic, and repeated himself frequently. Reminds you of your desktop or your TweetDeck, doesn't it?

But da Vinci's defenders point out that his sense of connectedness was so all-embracing that his observations are equally valid however they actually relate to one another. In other words, he didn't need to organize them by category or create an outline because he saw how everything connected to everything else.

And 360-degree thinking helps your board, committees, and staff leadership teams relate to each other and work together as a group. As you think about their interconnectedness, ask yourself these questions:

- What role does each person or group play?
- How are the roles interdependent?
- What are the advantages of the distribution of roles? What are the disadvantages?
- What happens to the dynamics under stress?
- What patterns have been handed down through the years in the culture of your association that affect the work of these groups?
- What are the primary forces outside the organization that affect the group dynamics?
- What were the dynamics like a year ago? Five years ago?
- How do the patterns of functioning you learned in this group affect the way you participate in other groups?
- If we had to draw a diagram of our board committee or staff leadership team as a system, what would it look like?

The management theorist movements in the 1980s and 1990s that focused on creating learning organizations and total quality management were an attempt to apply *connessione* thinking to organizations. Peter Senge, in his classic work *The Fifth Discipline* (1993), emphasized the complex, rapidly changing environments that organizations found themselves in and made the argument that new times necessitate new competencies. He believed that leaders need to cultivate the discipline of seeing the "whole" rather than the parts of our organizations, of seeing interrelationships rather than individual elements, and of seeing patterns of change rather than snapshots. "Reality is made up of circles, but we see straight lines," he said.

Association leaders will need to better identify the circles. They will need to understand the holistic nature of organizations and complex decision-making. Leading and making decisions in the future will require an increasingly holistic view, and the practice of 360-degree thinking will help them in this effort.

Information Filters

There is another way that 360-degree thinking can help association leaders see on all sides, and that is at a stage long before a decision must be made. The concept of *connessione,* looking at all things at all times, is especially powerful now because of the information vortex created by the endless amount of data we both generate and consume.

How can association leaders improve their ability to pay attention to all these things at once? Or more importantly, how can 360-degree thinkers see the whole picture and yet create rational mechanisms to organize data flow?

One way to address this dilemma is through the creation of idea filters. What kind of information do leaders need when using 360-degree thinking? Do leaders need to consider industry information, competitor information, best practices in association management, general business and economic news, as well as global developments if the association's scope extends to those interests? Leaders who think about these categories of information as filters are able to organize and access the most essential information at any given time. Interestingly, this is similar to the concept of creating a mechanism to handle Twitter flow, such as TweetDeck.

There is so much information that, even with filters, it is difficult to absorb everything all the time. However, successful association leaders use information filters to better understand the most relevant data they need. And the most effective chief staff officers inspire their boards to engage in 360-degree thinking as well. This enables the organization as a whole to benefit from a wider, broader, deeper, and more informed point of view.

No association or association leader can absorb and act on all information available to them, nor can or should they provide information to members without some sort of value-added filter. Effective associations serve as curators of conversations and distillers of information by looking around themselves at all times, absorbing information, putting their interpretation and perspectives on it in a way that members will find of value, and making it available through the association . This concept of curatorship is very powerful for associations, and in his book, *Curation Nation* (2011), Steve Rosenbaum describes this important role for organizations of all types.

But the most important aspect of 360-degree thinking is not just amassing information and being able to integrate or filter it. It is having the capacity to identify the interconnections and patterns that emerge from seemingly disjointed pieces of information.

One of the tools presented in this book is the leadership competency of powerful questions—the idea of asking deep, probing questions. It is through powerful questions that leaders identify patterns—patterns that emerge because leaders are able to see the interconnections between ideas.

For example, consider an association that is experiencing a decrease in membership renewal among a particular segment of its membership. The organization is simultaneously experiencing reduced attendance at education events among this demographic. Through competitive analysis, association leaders learn of a new group offering similar services to this category of membership. By identifying these interconnected pieces of information and asking what this data means, association leaders discover that this segment of membership is finding value from another organization, and their association is at risk of losing the demographic altogether. If leaders examined each piece of data in isolation, this insight may have been overlooked. However, by examining the data through powerful questions and looking at how data points interrelate, association leaders make a profound discovery.

Here is another example: 360-degree thinking also would have benefitted a trade association in which members did not have sufficient understanding of the interconnectedness of various segments of their industry. The association represented a segment of stakeholders within a larger food-related industry. In serving the very specific needs of its members, the association failed to see that the advocacy issues they were facing were increasingly similar to issues that a broader cross-section of that industry was dealing with as well. Because the association's membership represented an industry segment that was not only food-specific but also carried a set of beliefs related to the role and quality of the product, the association failed to see the possibilities of aligning themselves with others on issues of regulation that threatened to affect the industry as a whole.

The association's leaders could have benefited from 360-degree thinking by looking at the larger picture and understanding that future success on this policy issue would require a collaborative and coordinated effort, despite the perceived disconnect in values among the industry segments. As is explored in Chapter 6, people often fail to embrace and accept change because of underlying fears and assumptions. And the leaders of this organization clearly feared that their value sets would be compromised through collaboration with other industry segments. Consequently, they missed an opportunity to shape the future of their industry and to serve their members.

Whole-Brain Thinking

The notion of whole-brain thinking is an emerging concept in leadership research circles and has a distinct connection to the idea of 360-degree thinking. The concept of whole brain relates to how you naturally think, and the idea of 360-degree thinking relates to what to think about—in other words, what information, ideas, sources, and directions to focus on.

Each of us naturally thinks a certain way, has more interest in certain areas, and—above and beyond all—is most effective in certain ways. Understanding left- and right-brain thinking preferences can help association leaders better embrace the possibilities of 360-degree thinking.

Physiologically, the brain consists of two halves, or hemispheres. The right side of the brain looks at things in a visual way and is typically described as holistic or global. The left side first sees the details and puts them together to form the bigger picture and is typically considered analytic in approach. Both sides of the brain can reason, and we typically and unconsciously mix and match each side's abilities, resulting in a fully functional human brain. However, each of us has a dominant side, and we more often use the behaviors of that side. Therefore, awareness and understanding of our own brain preferences is helpful.

Regardless of which side of the brain is dominant for a particular individual, the brain finds it easier to process information if it is presented as an image rather than as words or numbers. The right hemisphere recognizes shapes and colors. The left side of the brain processes information in an analytical and sequential way and is more active when a person is reading a text or looking at a spreadsheet. Looking through a numerical table takes a lot of mental effort, but information presented visually can be grasped in a few seconds. The brain identifies patterns, proportions, and relationships to make instant subliminal comparisons.

For many years, the use of right-brain, intuitive thinking was discouraged in business circles. Executives and managers were encouraged to be left-brained, analytical, logical, data-driven, and detached from their emotions.

But leaders are seeing the value of increased use of right-brain thinking in business settings. In a *Psychology Today* blog article "Wired for Success" (June 1, 2010), Ray Williams observed, "A decade ago, we were enamored in the age of left-brain business. We were mesmerized by Six Sigma and ISO 9000 and spreadsheets and multilevel regulations and policies. We thought we could line-item budget our way to greatness, create shareholder value by tracking every employee's minute tasks, and employ a dress-code policy to conquer the marketplace. But it's become obvious that we may have reached the limits to analyzing processes, technology, and linear thinking." Williams notes that the right brain is gaining importance in the business world, and even in the corporate world, executives increasingly are talking about values, sustainability, and social responsibility. "Emotion, context, and meaning are becoming front-and-center."

Williams also notes that recent studies indicate a trend toward leaders' increased reliance on both left-brain analytical skills and right-brain intuitive feelings, which is known as whole-brain thinking. And he says that the latest brain science research has shown that it is virtually impossible to have entirely logical and analytical thinking and that emotions and experience are the key drivers for making decisions, not logic alone.

Although we use the terms right- and left-brain thinking here, consultant Jay McNaught, MBA, PhD, in his dissertation "How Baby-Boomer Experienced Leaders Use Intuition in Decision-Making" (Indiana Wesleyan University, April 2012), notes that more recent neuro-research no longer agrees on whether the right-brain type of thinking necessarily happens on the physical right side of the brain. Scientists are beginning to recognize that the left-brain/right-brain paradigm is limited. MRI imaging is showing that types of thinking are not really limited to one side of the brain or the other and, in fact, brain function happens in more variants than just these two sides.

In *The Whole Brain Business Book: Unlocking the Power of Whole-Brain Thinking in Organizations and Individuals* (1996), Ned Herrmann added an additional dimension and created four quadrants of thinking: "This four-quadrant model serves as an organizing principle of how the brain works: Each quadrant in the metaphor has a set of thinking characteristics associated with it. Quadrant A is labeled "upper left," and the thinking characteristics are logical, analytical, fact-based, and quantitative. Quadrant B is labeled "lower left," and the thinking characteristics are organized, sequential, planned, and detailed. Quadrant C is labeled "lower right," and the thinking characteristics are interpersonal, feeling-based, kinesthetic, and emotional. Quadrant D is labeled "upper right," and the thinking characteristics are holistic, intuitive, integrating, and synthesizing."

Despite this research, most of the popular management literature still uses left-brain and right-brain thinking as a metaphor. In *Thinking, Fast and Slow* (2011), Daniel Kahneman differentiates the two types of thinking as System 1 and System 2 thinking, emphasizing that several brain components are involved in both systems (not simply one half of the brain or the other).

Association leaders can benefit from accessing knowledge about their own brain portraits, not just thinking styles and preferences, but by understanding how they are hard-wired to think. If leaders don't understand that they are predisposed to only one brain preference, such as right- or left-brain thinking, they may not be able to embrace the full potential of 360-degree thinking. But a leader's natural preference for left- or right-brain thinking is not a limit in itself. It is the ability to be flexible in thinking preferences that is a critical skill. The most effective leaders recognize that they think in a certain way and attempt to surround themselves with people who think differently.

How can leaders better understand themselves and their thinking preferences? One instrument that may be helpful to association leaders in understanding their thinking portrait is the Neethling Brain Inventory or (NBI™), which identifies the thinking preferences of the individual. The NBI is an assessment tool that provides a descriptive, nonjudgmental analysis of an individual's thought preferences. It measures thinking preferences, not skills or ability in executing those preferences. It makes no judgments about whether any profile is better or worse than another but makes developmental recommendations based on the findings and helps leaders build their thinking and reaction capacity to be more adaptive to their environments. The NBI was developed after extensive international research on left- and right-brain functions. Kobus Neethling, under the research guidance of Professor Paul Torrance at the University of Georgia, developed the first NBI for adults. He then applied similar methodologies to develop a number of other whole-brain instruments. Ongoing research at a number of universities and institutes remains an essential part of whole-brain science, notes Herrmann. In Chapter 5, we present a case study exploring how the use of the NBI tool helped an association board better understand its own and each other's thinking styles, which resulted in better decisions and enhanced buy-in.

Whole-brain thinking is about more than just trying to solve problems; it's about trying to make sense of what we see and how we see it. It's more than making decisions; it's about creative puzzle solving—putting the pieces together and making meaning of what we see. It's about enhancing our ability to see the whole picture from 360 degrees.

How 360-Degree Thinking Would Have Helped One Professional Association

What happens when an association does not practice 360-degree thinking? Here is an example of an association that took a more piecemeal approach to developing its strategy and spent months working on a purpose statement and a set of principles that did not connect with a later articulation of the association's vision or potential.

A professional society that represents members engaged in a particularly detail-oriented professional specialty took a disjointed approach to developing the association's strategic plan. Over two years, the association's leaders engaged in separate retreat and committee activities to create different parts of the strategic plan.

One exercise created a vision that was designed to look 20 to 30 years into the future. Another exercise, executed a number of months later, looked at the association's bylaws and took the purpose statements from that document and adopted all of them into a mission statement. Another separate exercise involved setting short-term goals and tactics. Still another exercise focused on the culture of the association and the identification of values that might be inherent in the culture.

Although these activities sound like a reasonable way to address the development of strategy, there were a number of problems with this approach. First, each activity was done in a vacuum. The groups that were involved in developing short-term goals and tactics did not use the long-term vision as a basis for development. The group defining the association's purpose and the group working on its values were not the same. The bylaws committee, in fact, was also working on purpose because they consulted the bylaws for information, and no one on the bylaws committee had any direct connection to the board or senior staff.

Another problem with this approach was that after the creation of each of these strategy elements, the board voted separately on their acceptance, treating the adoption of each of these strategic elements as tasks on a list to be completed.

And the board itself was not actively engaged in producing any of the information. The strategic planning committee had been delegated most of the responsibility for these activities, with the exception of the bylaws committee that looked at purpose and a special anniversary vision committee that was focused on creating a goal to be used in conjunction with the association's celebration of this milestone.

As a result, the board saw its role as simply accepting the committee reports and approving the strategic plan bit by bit. Because this process happened over two years, one of the challenges was that board members who had supported and then approved one element, such as vision, were off the board by the time the committees were ready to bring other elements, such as short-term goals, to the board for approval. So there was little cohesion of vision, minimal organizational memory, and almost no thinking about how any of these elements affected or interrelated with the others.

Another problem with this approach was that because the board had not been actively engaged in creating these strategic elements, they had a very myopic view of the organization and its future threats and opportunities. Because they had not been directly engaged in environmental scanning, or SWOT analyses, or even in an active conversation about competitive strategy, their thinking was of the straight-ahead variety. They suffered from tunnel vision and were in denial about potential threats from other associations in the industry and other factors that were about to have a fundamental impact on their members' profession and the association itself. At the time, a competing organization had just presented an unwelcome offer to merge with this association, and not seeing the full picture of what was going on in the profession and the relative competitive environment of serving the members of this profession, this association's leaders chose not only to reject the other organization's offer but to do so in a way that alienated the other group and hindered the association's ability to engage in any future collaborative work with the group.

This association and its leaders could certainly have benefited from 360-degree thinking. If board members had been actively engaged in the development of all the strategic elements over a shorter time and with the benefit of active, frank discussion of the external factors, they would have had a much more realistic view of their situation and would have been better prepared to plan accordingly. They would have been able to see that values contribute to the execution of purpose and that purpose needs to be focused on the fundamental ongoing role that the organization will play. They would have understood that vision needs to be expressed in a way that articulates what the best possible outcome of the association's purpose suggests and describes what success would look like if there were no obstacles. They would have understood that an external view of the association, in the context of its competitive and industry environment, would have allowed them to see the potential barriers and challenges inherent in trying to achieve that vision. And if they had directly participated in the development of short-term goals, they would have understood that the goals need to be tied to the long-term vision, rather than having a vision that was unconnected to any actual work toward it that would result in incremental, measurable progress.

Because the association and its leaders were practicing heads down, tunnel-vision thinking, they had little understanding of the relevant external competitive environment in which they were operating. There was no sense of urgency, no imperative for change, and no real coordinated strategy to move forward. Unfortunately, they were placed in a position to be reactive at best. Practicing 360-degree thinking would have helped this board understand the larger environment in which it was operating and the profession the association was serving. It would have helped board members see patterns that suggested that their current path would not lead to future success, given the changes in the industry. In this particular industry, members' functions had become increasingly less specialized, and professionals with competing designations and other qualifications were being hired to do the work that this association's members had traditionally enjoyed exclusivity over. Engaging in 360-degree thinking would have helped the association's leaders be more open to change because they would have recognized that change in the industry was inevitable and that the association could have had a role in shaping, rather than responding to, the change. Such thinking would have helped this association serve its membership more effectively. But instead, this group missed an opportunity to lead its association and membership successfully into the future.

Thoughts to Consider About 360-Degree Thinking

- What kinds of information am I as an individual leader looking at all the time?
- Do my board members or I fall into tunnel vision?
- How aware am I of peripheral information?
- What are my information filters?
- Do my board and I have the capacity for *connessione?*
- How can I use reflective questions to step back and see patterns in this information and knowledge?
- Are my board and I aware of our individual or collective brain preferences?
- How can 360-degree thinking benefit me as a leader or my board or my organization?

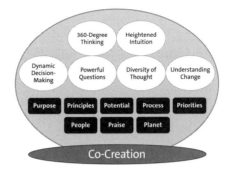

CHAPTER 2

Heightened Intuition

T HERE IS NO SHORTAGE of data available to association leaders today. According to Eric Schmidt, the CEO of Google, every two days as much information is created as was created in the first 2000 years of civilization. Today, the typical corporate user sends about 150 emails per day. Facebook now has nearly 1 billion active users that add more than 30 billion pieces of content each month.

But having more data does not necessarily lead to better decisions. The more available data, the more difficult it is to focus attention on the right things or to ascertain patterns, meaning, or full comprehension of the data. In Martin Greenberger's *Computers, Communication, and the Public Interest* (1971), Herbert Simon, a professor at Carnegie Mellon University, wrote in "Designing Organizations for an Information-Rich World," "Information consumes the attention of its recipients. Hence, a wealth of information creates a poverty of attention."

In *Blink* (2005), his popular book about decision-making, Malcolm Gladwell says, "We live in a world saturated with information. We have virtually unlimited amounts of data at our fingertips at all times, and we're well versed in the arguments about the dangers of not knowing enough and not doing our homework. But what I have sensed is an enormous frustration with the unexpected cost of knowing too much…. We have come to confuse information with understanding."

Have we confused information with understanding? When association leaders sit down to make decisions, what role do data play in driving the nature of the decision? How would decisions change if we stepped back and took a good look at what the data are actually indicating?

In the heavily data-driven environment in which association leaders are working and with the increased volume, speed, and complexity of decision-making required of board, staff, and volunteer workgroups, is it still reasonable to assume that either individual leaders or groups can make decisions based purely on data?

Probably not. For leaders to think, lead, and achieve in the future, intuition must play an increasingly more important role in the decision-making process and will need to serve as a balance for a heavily data-driven environment. An emerging and essential leadership competency for success must be the ability for both individuals and groups to develop heightened intuition and to balance data with their internal compasses. It will be increasingly important for leaders to effectively integrate intuition into the decision-making process, rather than relying solely on data. No one individual can know everything, and the more complex an issue is, the less that data alone can shed light on the best answer. Leaders' ability to heighten their own intuition and to balance data with intuition will lead to better decisions and more successful organizations.

Greater use of intuition in decision-making has three benefits: 1) It helps guide leaders to recognize important issues that may affect the organization; 2) It can help leaders in building their emotional intelligence by allowing them to more effectively understand people's innate motivations in any given work or decision-making situation; and 3) It is an important component for effective dynamic decision-making (as detailed in Chapter 3).

The ability to look beyond the data, balance a variety of ambiguities, and come upon the right solution, sometimes almost unconsciously, will benefit association leaders and their organizations. If association leaders, both volunteers and staff, were able to better integrate intuition into decision-making processes, it is conceivable that many decisions could be made more quickly and with a greater degree of buy-in, resulting in a greater sense of connection to both the process and the outcomes.

In this chapter, we will explore the concept of heightened intuition both in individuals and groups and provide strategies for association leaders to improve their intuitive skills. In the following chapter we will talk more specifically about the process of integrating intuition into individual and organizational decision-making.

Jay E. McNaught collaborated on this chapter and offers comments throughout that are based on his recent research into the role of intuition in decision-making for his dissertation, "How Baby-Boomer Experienced Leaders Use Intuition in Decision-Making," (Indiana Wesleyan University, April 2012).

Defining *Intuition*

Intuition is sometimes described as a gut feeling we have about whether something is good or bad, or an inner voice that makes suggestions to us in various situations. Often, intuition comes to us quickly. When we are faced with a situation or decision, sometimes we just instantly know what to do—or not to do.

Intuition is used to bring forward ideas, images, and possibilities or to find ways out of a blocked situation, using a process that is mostly unconscious. Intuition has been studied for many years. In *Psychological Types* (1921), Carl Gustav Jung defined intuition as "perception via the unconscious." He developed a theory that is now used in the Myers-Briggs Type Indicator (MBTI), with the categories of thought processes including intuiting, sensing, thinking, feeling, perceiving, and judging. Personality types that fall under the *intuiting* category rely on patterns and impressions as opposed to information gathered through the five senses, although in actuality, the *feeling* preference more closely aligns with the definition of intuitive decision-making than intuiting. Intuiting in MBTI is more about how individuals take in information, not how they process it.

Writing in the 1970s, Seymour Epstein, PhD, a University of Massachusetts psychologist, developed his "cognitive experiential self" theory. In it, he points out that human beings process information through two systems. Just as we learn things consciously all the time—the cognitive part of the theory—we also learn things experientially, without realizing we've learned them. "Intuition is just the things we've learned without realizing we've learned them. And sometimes they're useful. Sometimes they're maladaptive," Epstein says. For example, a person who has learned through past experiences to like and trust other people might have very different social intuitions than someone who's learned to fear and distrust others.

What else do we know about intuition? Sadler-Smith and Shefy in "The Intuitive Executive: Understanding and Applying 'Gut Feel' in Decision-Making," *Academy of Management Executive,* 18(4), 2004, offer these observations about intuition: "Intuition is a composite phenomenon that incorporates expertise and feeling.... It is not simply educated ("smart") guessing.... It resides at a level below consciousness, arises cognitively and affectively, and is manifested as a 'hunch' or 'gut feel.' These feelings may be associated with images or narratives or an abstract feeling of certitude about the rightness or wrongness of a course of action."

Malcolm Gladwell recently popularized the concept of intuition in *Blink* (2005), although he preferred not to use the term. Arguing that the human brain performs processing functions that individuals are totally unaware of, he references those processing functions as the "adaptive unconscious." Adaptive unconscious is a set of mental processes influencing judgment and decision-making in a way that is inaccessible to introspective awareness. The adaptive unconscious is distinguished from conscious processing in a number of ways, including being faster, effortless, more focused on the present, and less flexible.

So this theory suggests that intuition is something that often seems to emerge from somewhere within us, and it is something we usually have a strong feeling about. Intuition is about thought, but it is also about emotion, values, innate beliefs, and assumptions.

Let's explore the concept of intuition a bit further to illuminate its usefulness.

Characteristics of Intuition

When talking about intuition, we are describing something that is known, perceived, understood, or believed by instinct, feelings, or human nature, without actual evidence, rather than by use of conscious thought, reason, or rational processes. This does not imply that intuitive decision-making is irrational. Instead, the explanation for a choice may not always be directly available through conscious or logical thought (although some leaders, upon making an intuitive decision, are later able to determine the path their unconscious took in arriving at the decision and that serves as additional validation).

Brain research has examined parts of the brain that work simultaneously with our conscious thought processes, acting as parallel intelligent systems. These systems will create responses (sometimes emotional) that compete with each other in determining a person's response. When guided by experience with a previous pattern, these responses could be considered the result of intuition.

In his dissertation, McNaught defined intuitive decision-making as "rapid decision-making, done without conscious deliberation, that results in affectively charged judgments." He based this definition in part on the work of Dane and Pratt, who, in their article "Exploring Intuition and Its Role in Managerial Decision-Making," *Academy of Management Review*, (32)(1), 2007, defined a series of characteristics of intuition:

- Intuiting occurs outside conscious thought. We are not always aware that we are even engaging our intuition. It is like a running narrative on the periphery of our conscious minds.

- Intuiting involves making holistic connections. According to Dane and Pratt: "It involves a process in which environmental stimuli are matched with deeply held (nonconscious) categories, patterns, or features." This means that a wide variety of information, signals, senses, beliefs, factors, and judgments can become part of the decision-making process, and the more an association leader is able to think in a holistic, multidimensional, nonlinear manner, the greater the ability to integrate a wide variety factors in any kind of decision.

• Intuiting is faster than rational decision-making processes. There is no question that the speed in which decisions need to be made in association leadership is important and will continue to be critical. Boards that have adopted a data-driven, process-heavy methodology for decision-making may take entire board meetings just to digest the data to everyone's satisfaction, and then the actual business of decision-making has to be carried over from meeting to meeting to meeting, thus delaying the necessary speed of decision-making and action.

• Intuitive decisions are affectively charged, meaning that emotions are involved. What is the role of emotion in association leadership and decision-making? We have moved in recent years to data-driven decision-making in hopes of depoliticizing the process, ensuring that rational knowledge and not individual leader preferences drives the decision. These actions are certainly well-intentioned, and many associations have made good progress in developing competency in this area. But a deficiency in the data-driven approach is that through the crush of data analysis and rational and detailed discussions, somehow we may have eliminated a critical component in our decision-making—that of an emotional connection to the decision or outcome.

Link to Emotional Intelligence

Despite long-held cultural assumptions in many organizations, emotions are no longer taboo in the workplace. Emotional intelligence is a leadership concept that has been growing in popularity. J.D. Mayer and Paul Salovey, in *Emotional Development and Emotional Intelligence: Implications for Educators* (1997), characterized it as "the ability to perceive emotions, to access and generate emotions so as to assist thought, to understand emotions and emotional knowledge, and to reflectively regulate emotions so as to promote emotional and intellectual growth."

Daniel Goleman has popularized the notion of emotional intelligence in his books *Leadership: The Power of Emotional Intelligence* (2011) and *Primal Leadership* (2002). His research supports the theory that decisions are better, performance more substantial, and leadership more compelling if leaders are actually emotionally invested in their decisions.

In *Primal Leadership*, Goleman identified four domains of emotional intelligence: self-awareness (recognizing what we're feeling at any given moment), self-management (managing those feelings), social awareness (understanding what others are feeling), and relationship management (putting it all together by developing healthy workplace relationships).

Our identification of heightened intuition as a critical leadership competency aligns with Goleman's research findings, and especially with the first domain—self-awareness, which he says is a basis for good intuition and good decision-making. Building a heightened sense of intuition helps leaders tap into their own internal compasses in a powerful way.

Many researchers believe that emotional intelligence (EQ) may be more important for a leader's success than the leader's actual intelligence (IQ). The ability to accurately "read" or assess the emotions of others is a critical component of emotional intelligence.

Leaders' Use of Intuition in Decision-Making

So what do we know about the use of intuition by association leaders today? Is it in use? Does it add value? Why is it an emerging leadership competency? The following content draws on interviews conducted by McNaught with senior leaders in a variety of corporate and nonprofit environments as well as our own research into the perceptions of association leaders. What we learned from them about the use of intuition is characterized in clusters of focus below.

Intuition is not always recognized. One of the dynamics we observed is that leaders often use intuition but don't refer to it by name. For example, the CEO of a professional society said, "People want to apply their experience in making a decision but may not call it intuition. The health of our organization depends on my paying attention to what's going on around us, and although I don't call it intuition, I use my past experience, see patterns, and listen to my own internal compass as much as I pay attention to the data we've collected."

A staff leader in a local government agency told us, "We are the only species that doesn't listen to our intuition. I am in a world that is very focused on data. In our department, we are helping people listen to their intuition more. Especially in dealing with people, there are a lot of things that aren't said. You have to use your intuition, what you've learned over time, and your experience to help you understand what the data are telling you. You have to understand the impact of implementing a decision based on the data alone, which may not always yield the best result."

The role of patterns. Leaders spoke of having a sense of what's going on around them, nourished not just by seeing the data but by sensing the patterns inherent in that data. "Following our intuition causes us to ask questions," notes Carrie Mattingly, utilities director of the City of San Luis Obispo, California, and state president of the California Water Environment Association. "And if we ask enough questions of enough people, we can identify patterns in the conversations. And those patterns are useful in identifying needs or problems, and they are critical in making decisions. The key is to ask questions and listen. Sometimes member needs don't show up in data or in surveys, but they are recognized as patterns in conversations."

Mattingly also notes that a supportive organizational culture is essential to the use of heightened intuition. "We need to give people permission to speak about the unspeakable. Give permission to float new ideas. Group intuition can be seen by giving people permission to think and share what they are thinking. You need a connector in your organization, someone who connects the dots between peoples' intuitions, someone who can listen for patterns."

History and experience. Intuition has a lot to do with history and experience and drawing upon those as a balance to data in decision-making.

One corporate leader McNaught interviewed noted that his experience led him to value the role of experience in intuition. Very few of the decisions that he makes are decisions that he had not experienced before. "In other words, if I've experienced something exactly the same—or reasonably the same—obviously it drives a lot of that intuition." He explained that when a decision arose where he lacked previous experience, he would move toward a more rational decision-making process. "If it's something that is a new experience for me then, obviously, either my comfort with the scenario or the outcome is not as sure-footed and so again will require a good amount of data in that regard But sometimes experience allows me to make a decision when little data is available. Experience gives me the confidence to 'trust my gut' because I have experienced similar situations in the past. "It's not infallible. We are a product of our experiences and the past decisions we've made, right or wrong."

But history is not always an accurate predictor of the future. Christopher Seiz, executive director of the Long Beach Island Foundation of the Arts and Sciences, told us, "Sometimes feedback is based on historical perspective rather than the impression of the here and now. As a result, we have to interpret the data. Sometimes people remember things the way they were rather than see them the way they are now.

Complexity and the role of creativity. One of the leaders we interviewed said, "Simple decisions can often be made with knowledge-based decision-making; however, the more complex the issue is, the more important it is to integrate intuition into the decision-making process. Sometimes, intuition can cut through the complexity of an issue."

This leader noted that she has read Daniel Kahneman's *Thinking, Fast and Slow* (2011) and sees a correlation between the book and the concept of heightened intuition. For example, she notes that Google allocates a percentage of employees' time to creative thinking and innovation. They have ideas meetings where employees discuss their thoughts and create new products and services.

Values. We know that values—both individual and organizational—play a key role in intuition. One leader identified organizational values as an important filter for intuitive decisions.

In his organization, he posted signs with the list of organizational values. He refers to the values when making decisions that affect the organization or colleagues within the organization. He says, "So you've got to think about all those kinds of decisions. That's why those values are on the wall. In the decision-making process, you'd better be sure that you're consistent with them. Because if you're not consistent with them, then what happens? You shouldn't have even put those values statements up there, because nobody's adhering to them. And everybody realizes that the values don't mean anything to the leaders."

In a similar fashion, another association leader described values as a "screen" through which he sifts his decisions: "I think you have a sense…of the kind of the core beliefs and values that we're trying to develop and embed within the organization. So, for example, one screen that I will try to put things through is how this affects customer centricity? So there has been more of a conscious effort to put a lot of these decisions through that screen. I would say we're putting a lot more rigor in that particular screen."

One leader identified an accumulation of "rules" that she has developed over time to guide her with her intuitive decision-making. Even though she said that she could not consciously list the rules, the rules appear to be based on her values: "At the end of the day it would come around to core questions: Is it ethical? Is it honest? Is it right? Does it create value (for the shareholder in this case)? So those would be the sorts of things that I think about. Could I recite the specific rules? I'd probably be hard-pressed to do that."

Shared Intuition

We explored the need for individual association leaders to build a greater sense of their own intuition. But what about intuition in groups? What about the use of intuition in board decision-making? Is there such a thing as shared intuition?

For many years, consultant advice has helped associations eliminate damaging political dynamics in decision-making by using a knowledge-based decision-making model. Many associations have integrated this model into their governance culture and have mastered it. But there is now something new to strive for in this area. The next frontier is for boards and work groups to build shared intuition as a group to enhance their decision-making processes and outcomes.

Researchers Drury and Kitsopoulos made observations in their article "Do You Still Believe in The Seven Deadly Myths?" in *Consulting to Management* (March 2005) about intuition in groups: "When a group makes decisions, people's values, alternatives, and expectations interact, which makes it a less rational process. Yet this 'irrational' decision-making process often works best because it maximizes motivation and commitment. If management consultants don't understand and accept the irrational part in us all, they won't reach optimal solutions."

Sports teams have shared intuition. Consider a lob pass in basketball. The point guard and the center have a moment of eye communication and a sense of how to time the pass and the leap perfectly to provide the slam-dunk. It is shared intuition that tells them what to do and where to go.

Research suggests that intuition can be expanded to groups, and this has implications for association boards. Researcher Dee Ann Kline, in a chapter titled "Intuitive Team Decision-Making," in *How Professionals Make Decisions* (2005), comments on teams using an intuitive decision-making process:

> When a team is faced with a decision event, they intuitively compare the event to the knowledge in the shared mental models they have developed [group norms, agreements, values, goals]. If the event can be understood by this comparison, the team implicitly knows the solution and is able to rapidly reach intuitive consensus. Cohesive teams have a shared mental model of behaviors that team members expect one another to exhibit, such as honesty, trust, respect for others, accountability, empathy, belonging, and open communication, as well as shared commitment to goals that are closely aligned with the organization's vision or philosophy.

Although Kline conducted research on work teams in a hospital setting, these findings can be applied to association leadership teams as well. Many association boards have already established behavioral norms such as discussion guidelines, codes of conduct, and other operating procedures. If a board has also truly institutionalized these, has actually developed the ability to conduct its business routinely within these norms, they already have an important foundation for the development of shared intuition. Another similarity is the existence of a shared commitment to a strategic long-range plan, or specific vision and goal statements. Many association boards have articulated and committed to these elements, and those can serve as shared mental models.

Another element of intuitive team decision-making is characterized by an ability to speed up decision-making and quickly reach a decision.

Association boards have less and less time for complex data-driven decision-making processes, but many still spend significant time pouring over voluminous amounts of data, still not making optimal decisions. The primary change in the board decision-making process with the integration of shared intuition is the laborious step of analyzing each piece of data, each choice or option, each pro and con, and each risk and consequence. What happens in a board that makes a shared intuitive decision is so much more powerful than practical consensus. They all immediately know it is right. Consensus is immediately formed because their decisions are based not just on the process of analyzing the data but on a connection to values, principles, and personal intuition; because it connects with them on a deeper level and they feel a greater sense of ownership in it. An association board that has developed a sense of shared intuition can make decisions in a fairly quick time frame, without extensive data analysis, discussion, or advocacy, and the resulting decisions can have broader buy-in and agreement. But shared intuition goes beyond just defining shared values. It is an almost unconscious process where clear consensus on the right path seems to emerge out of nowhere, devoid of laborious data analysis and potentially divisive advocacy.

Sometimes groups may not even plan for or be aware of the fact that the decision has been made in an intuitive manner. The decision is sometimes described as "something that just happened," an agreement to just act on something that the team collectively and immediately knew, and consensus was reached with limited discussion of the decision event. Discussions and evaluations play a role in intuitive team decision-making; however, they largely take place after decisions are made. Intuitive decision-making is followed by a period in which the team both validates the decision and concurrently plans for implementation. If team members suggest different courses of action regarding implementation, they may discuss them, but the fact that the decision has been reached makes this dialogue more efficient and less potentially divisive.

One of the most important factors in shared intuition is the understanding that happens among group members. Shared intuition is advanced by incorporating shared values, brain and thinking preferences, and emotional components, and it places a heightened focus on boards as people, not as mere data analysis panels. If board members were to invest more time in understanding their thinking styles and preferences, they would not only build trust but potentially build greater capacity for shared intuition.

How can moving to shared intuition in their decision-making benefit association leaders and their boards? For many boards, there can never be enough data. There will never be enough time for dialogue and discussion. For some boards, dialogue and discussion will never lead them to a decision. Shared intuition provides a way to get unstuck, to know each other as individuals, to be able to communicate on a level where they're actually able to listen to each other, understand, and validate each other's issues and concerns.

For many associations, values have become nothing but text in their strategic plans. Many boards have not spent sufficient time understanding how and why values should guide their decision-making. A greater focus on values has the potential to be an enfranchising, cohesive factor. It is one of the only things that can bring a group together. Along with shared intuition, common values can ensure a focus on the greater good and the sacrifice of individual self-interest.

Case Study of Shared Intuition on an Association Board

How does shared intuition work in practice? Following is an example of how one association board made a critical decision using shared intuition.

The Association of Pet Dog Trainers (APDT) is a professional society of individuals who train dogs and other companion animals. Founded in 1993, the South Carolina-based association serves as a forum for education and knowledge exchange. A staff of five serves more than 6,000 members worldwide and a five-member board governs the association.

At a recent meeting, two board members were continuing, and three were new. In addition to covering the typical board orientation discussions about roles and responsibilities at the beginning of the meeting, the APDT board engaged in team development related to each individual's personality preferences and thinking styles. Using the Needling Brain Instrument assessment process, the board members were able to gain deeper understanding, both individually and collectively, about whether their thinking preferences were right brain, left brain, whole brain, intuitive, analytical, detail oriented, and/or big picture.

A facilitator helped them explore the assessment results individually and then share the information with each other. A group profile was created to give the board a sense of its collective strengths and preferences. The dialogue on these issues seemed to immediately create a greater sense of openness and a shared understanding of each other's perspective.

The APDT board continued the meeting with its business agenda and the next day addressed several issues of program strategy. Discussion began about what to do with a particular business line that was supported by some members but did not align well with the association's future direction. All was quiet in the board room until one board member said, "My sense is that we really need to get out of this business."

Everyone looked around, and as individual board members began to express similar views, it quickly became evident that consensus had been reached. There was no extensive, drawn-out discussion of multiple choices, pros and cons, or advantages and disadvantages.

There was no questioning of the sufficiency of the data. All board members had come to the meeting having thoroughly read the background materials. But upon opening the discussion, the group simply and simultaneously realized that there was one right path. They were able to achieve shared intuition in this decision-making process and were comfortable with both the process and the outcome. There were no feelings of compromise, of having settled, or of having lost.

Nancy Alexander, a Connecticut-based senior consultant for Ideas for Action, LLC, describes shared intuition decisions this way: "When a group arrives at a decision through shared intuition, there's a palpable feeling in the room. Even if there are still open questions about how the decision will be implemented, there is a collective feeling of peace and calm and, above all, connectedness with each other. The matter feels "settled," but not in the sense of "settling" for something less than possible. In fact, it feels like more than was thought possible. And it doesn't feel like compromise, the kind where you can feel the dissatisfaction and disconnectedness after the decision is made. You can tell that each person in the room has connected with the organization's shared values, purpose, and priorities and has honored those rather than a personal agenda."

Indeed, following its decision, the APDT board began discussion about guidelines for staff and committee implementation. There were some concerns about the decision itself—political, financial, and communications issues. But with each passing minute and with each point that was raised, all board members became more and more invested in the decision. The board member who was serving as the liaison to the affected program committee and would need to be the primary communicator of the board's decision voiced some concern not about the decision itself but about the communication of the decision. Despite the fact that this was her first APDT board meeting, she felt a sufficient level of trust in the room to articulate her concerns to the group. The board understood and valued her perspective and assured her that they would wholeheartedly support her communication about the decision the board made.

Because there was agreement and sufficient dialogue, rather than debate followed by a divisive vote, all board members finished the discussion with a sense of buy-in and satisfaction and were able to support the decision when it ultimately was presented to the membership.

Earlier in the meeting, the board members had reviewed the association's strategic plan. There had been a reaffirmation of the association's purpose, values, and vision. The discussion about purpose brought forth a renewed understanding of the primary focus of the association. Following the programmatic decision, board members pointed to the fact that the earlier articulation of purpose had been influential, essential, and instrumental in helping them quickly and intuitively make the decision about this particular program business line as it related to the centrality of the association and its mission.

The power of shared intuition is evident here. Board members and staff together more clearly articulated and acted on the purpose of their organization. They came to a shared understanding of principles, which included beliefs, values, and assumptions, and articulated a shared vision, what the organization was seeking to accomplish should it reach its full potential.

All this discussion brought them together in a shared view, which helped to focus and streamline the discussion. And the opportunity to know and understand each other individually on a deeper level as a result of the thinking profiles assessment earlier in the meeting helped them to quickly build a deeper level of trust and understanding.

Simply because of its size, a board of five can achieve this level of understanding faster than a board of 20 or more members. The APDT board meets face to face quarterly, and engages in frequent telephone conference calls. Many association boards do not have the ability to spend this much time together. But time together and group size are not among the most important dimensions of achieving shared intuition. More important is greater understanding of each other as individuals; a high level of trust; shared focus on purpose, values, and vision; and a supportive board culture. Regardless of size, boards can and should work toward these goals.

Many associations have made great progress in evolving positive governance cultures, and have developed the ability to sustain them over time, through multiple years and successive leaders. Some boards have even reached the point of believing that they have accomplished all that they can in terms of evolving governance and that the role of each new leadership team is to merely sustain the successes gained in this area.

But we believe that the potential for shared intuition is the next level of possibility for these boards and is something new to strive for.

The use of shared intuition does not obviate the need for effective data collection and analysis, knowledge sharing, and extended dialogue. Boards still need background knowledge and insight related to association management on key decisions. Staff still must provide the knowledge and perspectives that integrate all the competencies. Dialogue still needs to happen among the board members to gain greater understanding to allay fears and concerns and to ensure that they are all on the same page. Board and staff leadership teams still must engage in collaborative dialogue. But decisions that are reached through shared intuition have the potential to move association leadership teams efficiently and effectively to true co-creation—full investment in both the process and the outcome of decision-making.

Shared Intuition Is Not Groupthink

Shared intuition is not groupthink. Psychologist Irving Janis coined that term in his book *Victims of Groupthink: A Psychological Study of Foreign Policy Decisions and Fiascoes* (1972): "The act or practice of reasoning or decision-making by a group, especially when characterized by uncritical acceptance or conformity to prevailing points of view." Groupthink occurs when the pressure to conform within a group interferes with that group's analysis of a problem and causes poor group decision-making. Individual creativity, uniqueness, and independent thinking are lost in the pursuit of group cohesiveness, as are the advantages that can sometimes be obtained by making a decision as a group—bringing different sources of ideas, knowledge, and experience together to solve a problem. Groupthink can also refer to the tendency of groups to agree with powerful, intimidating bosses.

The concept of groupthink provides a good explanation of why groups (and boards) sometimes make poor decisions. Indeed, groups are supposed to be better than individuals at making complex decisions because a variety of differing perspectives are brought to light in discussions. Group members, including association boards, not only serve to bring new ideas into the discussion but also act as error-correcting mechanisms. If there is a healthy atmosphere in the boardroom, board members can question each other in a way that helps to illuminate understanding of data and insights and does not result in personal challenges or attacks.

Groups can also provide social support, which is especially critical for new ideas. In the best associations, board members play important roles in not only generating new ideas but championing them. But when new perspectives are rejected, it is hard to correct errors. And if the social support is geared toward supporting the group's "accepted wisdom," things that block change or innovation, the elements that can make a group a more effective decision-maker than an individual can become inverted, and the group may actually end up making worse decisions!

If it is practiced in conjunction with the other emerging competencies described in this book, shared intuition will not result in groupthink. Groupthink is defined in terms of acceptance or conformity to prevailing points of view, but shared intuition, when practiced with competencies such as diversity of thought, powerful questions, and 360-degree thinking, ensures that whatever amount of dialogue is deemed necessary by the group, the dialogue will be rich in ideas and diverse viewpoints.

Shared intuition welcomes diverse thinking, and the end result is not a surface-level, politically based exercise in conformity but a collaborative agreement that comes from the collective processing of relevant data and perspectives, a deeper sense of articulated and espoused shared values, and comfort with the decision.

When a board is engaged in discussion about whether to take a particular policy position, for example, it has an obligation to explore all the relevant data and choices. Using a process that is familiar to many boards, this kind of dialogue would begin with a clarifying discussion of the data, to ensure that everyone has relatively equal knowledge of the particular issue.

The next part of the discussion would involve an analysis of the possible choices, although this may be included in the background paper that the board had been asked to review prior to the meeting.

The next step gets complicated. Some boards, despite this open dialogue, would simply end the discussion with a vote, and the majority would prevail. Other boards might take time to poll each member and understand where their concerns are, what "deal breakers" might exist for whom, and then try to reach a compromise decision that doesn't inflame anyone.

In some boards, the pressure to conform (as groupthink is defined) may occur. One board used a simple group process tool to take straw votes before final vote. If board members totally supported the idea and would unequivocally vote for it, they were asked to raise their thumbs in the up position. If they could support the decision, but still had some personal reservations, they were asked to raise their thumbs sideways. If they harbored fundamental concerns about the decision that would not allow them to fully support it and move forward, they were asked to turn their thumbs down.

While the "thumbs up" approach may feel like an effective group decision-making tool, it actually can contribute to groupthink if not used in a collaborative way.

In some boards, group members who voted thumbs down were pressured to change their vote not just to thumbs sideways but to thumbs up. In other words, the pressure to reach unilateral and unequivocal agreement was there. But in the interest of coming to a decision and moving forward, those who still had legitimate concerns about the decision would probably feel disenfranchised. Do we really want boards that routinely make unanimous decisions?

The better message to the board would be that it is acceptable to vote thumbs sideways, thereby preserving the right and the comfort level of each board member to raise future issues that result in rich dialogue and shared decision-making. We believe this is where individual values and intuition play an important role in a decision-making process. Pressuring a board toward unanimity invalidates the gut-level concerns that some members may have.

Decisions made with shared intuition can include discussion of data and evaluation of choices, fears, and concerns, but there should be no pressure toward unanimity. As boards build a greater sense of shared understanding, they can even learn to anticipate each other's concerns and compensate for them by reaching positions that would have taken much dialogue and compromise to reach before.

A heightened sense of intuition can help association leaders develop 360-degree thinking. In terms of intuitive awareness, association leaders need to develop and exercise intuition in assessing what to notice and where to focus attention. How can association leaders better sense where to center their attention? As one leader told us, data alone doesn't define strategy.

A heightened sense of intuition can assist association leaders in developing frames through which to view the organization and its data. We referred to this in the last chapter as "filters." In their book *Reframing Organizations* (1991), Bolman and Deal define frames as "... both windows on the world and lenses that bring the world into focus. Frames filter out some things while allowing others to pass through easily. Frames help us to order experience and decide what action to take."

Developing a heightened sense of intuition is important because it helps us understand what data we should collect, illuminate the data, make meaning, and create deeper understanding. The ability of association leaders to develop greater awareness of their intuition as well as a sense of shared intuition will enable them to better integrate data, stimuli, and information. Linear, data-driven decision-making must make way for holistic, interconnected, intuitive thought.

Sadler-Smith and Shefy, in "The Intuitive Executive: Understanding and Applying 'Gut Feel' in Decision-Making," *Academy of Management Executive*, 18(4), 2004, point out that the working environment and organizational culture can either support or suppress the use of intuitive decision-making. "The concomitant danger is that if intuition is continually suppressed, it may cease to operate or may be driven underground."

Burke and Miller, in "Taking the Mystery Out of Intuitive Decision-Making," *Academy of Management Executive*, 13(4), 1999, encourage organizations to establish cultures conducive to intuitive decision-making. "If an organization's work environment, leadership, political climate, and socialization processes do not support the use of intuition, then many employees will rely solely on objective methods and discount lessons learned from their personal database of experience."

The Use of Intuition Does Not Come Without Controversy

We must acknowledge that the role of intuition in decision-making is still controversial. Eric Bonabeau, writing in a May 2003 *Harvard Business Review* article, "Don't Trust Your Gut," stated, "Detached from rigorous analysis, intuition is a fickle and undependable guide—it is as likely to lead to disaster as to success. And while some have argued that intuition becomes more valuable in highly complex and changeable environments, the opposite is actually true."

Intuitive decision-making has the potential for error. The intuitive decision-making process might lead individuals and groups to overlook alternatives and, therefore, miss an even better solution. But even in a data-driven process, leaders may base decisions on inaccurate or incomplete information, and prejudices may overrule facts.

A mystique is associated with business leaders who make quick decisions and appear to rely heavily on their intuition. In his autobiography, *Jack: Straight from the Gut* (2001), Jack Welch credits quick and decisive decision-making as a key to his success at General Electric:

> I learned in a hundred ways that I rarely regretted acting but often regretted not acting fast enough. I could scarcely remember a time when I said, "I wish I'd taken six more months to study something before making a decision." I think acting decisively on people, plants, and investments was one of the reasons I got out of the pile very early at GE. Yet 40 years later when I retired, one of my great regrets was that I didn't act fast enough on many occasions. When I asked myself, "How many times should I have held off on a

decision?" versus, "How many times do I wish I'd made that move faster?" I inevitably found that the latter won almost every time.

In *The Power of Intuition: How to Use Your Gut Feelings to Make Better Decisions at Work* (2004), Gary Klein reflects on the role of intuition in decision-making and identifies the following potential issues:

- *Flawed information.* Intuition decision-making will respond quickly to inaccurate, insufficient, unreliable, or incomplete information based on patterns from previous experiences.

- *Short-term emotional bias.* Cognitive research has shown that even experts' decisions are influenced by unrelated emotions during the time of making a decision.

- *Insufficient consideration of alternatives.* Intuition generally relies on pattern recognition and will point to solutions that have worked well with the current perceived pattern. This will limit considered options even though you may be dealing with a new decision situation that might require a novel or unique solution.

- *Prejudices.* Emotions help form our intuition and can allow flawed experiences to overrule sound facts and evidence.

- *Lack of openness.* Every person has a different experience base that provides the platform for their intuitions. Given that one's intuition is not easily explained, it is difficult to use intuition in a group context.

- *Inappropriate application.* People who have good experience, expertise, and intuition in one area can become overconfident and apply their intuition in an unfamiliar or unrelated area. This also includes using "rules of thumb" that may not match the needs of the current decision context.

Writing in a blog on www.Gladwell.com titled "What is *Blink* About?" Gladwell notes that despite the value of improving our intuitive abilities, we are still "innately suspicious of this kind of rapid cognition. We live in a world that assumes that the quality of a decision is strictly related to the time and effort that went into making it." Gladwell shares his concern about even using the word *intuition* but still praises the need for developing competency in rapid cognition:

> You could also say that *Blink* is a book about intuition, except that I don't like that word. In fact it never appears in *Blink.* Intuition strikes me as a concept we use to describe emotional reactions, gut feelings—thoughts and impressions that don't seem entirely rational. But I think that what goes on in that first two seconds is perfectly rational. It's thinking—it's just thinking that moves a little faster and operates a little more mysteriously than the kind of deliberate, conscious decision-making that we usually associate with "thinking." In *Blink* I'm trying to understand those two seconds. What is going on inside our heads when we engage in rapid cognition? When are snap judgments good and when are they not? What kinds of things can we do to make our powers of rapid cognition better?

What Leaders Can Do to Improve Their Capacity for Shared Intuition

Because communication is necessary for the development of strong shared mental models, boards seeking to develop shared intuition will need to strengthen their basic communication skills, such as active listening, dialogue, and articulation of personal viewpoints by focusing on the content and not the person.

Once these skills are in place, boards can be taught to use dialogue to question assumptions and develop a deeper understanding of one another's viewpoints, roles, and experiences. With this understanding, they will begin to establish norms and come to agreement about the values they expect one another to exemplify. They will devise and commit to communication routines that support and enhance existing communication channels.

First, boards will need to develop higher levels of trust. In *The Will to Govern Well* (2002), Jean Frankel, Paul Meyer, and Glenn Tecker identified three elements that must be present to develop and sustain a culture of trust: the need for agreement on how success is defined collectively, open access to information, and confidence in the competency and commitment of partners in a leadership team. These same factors must be in place for boards to develop and practice shared intuition, and the good news for associations is that many have been working toward the development of a sustained culture of trust for many years. Understanding the associated risks of decisions is also something that many boards have worked toward. The data-driven, knowledge-based approach to governance and decision-making has enabled many boards to identify and analyze a variety of factors affecting decisions, and the process of determining whether there is missing or uncertain data has helped associations more fully understand and manage risk. Using this competency as part of shared intuition represents a next step for these boards.

Recognizing when intuitive decisions are possible is a newer competency that we have seen few boards develop. Many groups are still uncomfortable with ambiguity, still uneasy about risk, and not always willing to act in the absence of hard data.

Shared intuition will require a leap of faith for some boards. It will require boards to reach a greater comfort level with uncertainty, have the ability to maintain focus despite a multiplicity of solutions, have confidence in their actions despite little previous precedent, and be comfortable acting in shorter timeframes. Given that the environment is evolving for associations both in the general business world and in their professional, industry, or cause-related areas of focus and will continue to yield large amounts of data for analysis, hard data alone will not likely be the sole source for predicting the future in uncertain time. The need for shared intuition in the future will increase.

We have observed that boards that have achieved shared intuition have developed the following individual and group competencies to improve their decision-making processes:

- **Listen more effectively.** Improved listening will ensure that a greater amount of situational information is considered by participants in a shared decision-making process. The better informed the pattern is, the more likely that intuition will provide a solution well matched to the problem, challenge, or opportunity, and the more effective listeners leaders are, the more information they will absorb. Anyone who has taken any type of communication skills training knows the importance of good listening, but practicing it well is less common. Listening skills are important to effective board process but essential to shared intuition in decision-making. In Chapter 4 we discuss powerful questions as one of the six emerging competencies, and improved listening skills are an important part of that competency. Boards and staffs will need improved listening skills not only to gain a greater connection with their intuition but also to execute all the competencies and foundations in this book. As much as leaders need to develop these skills, shared intuition is also often helped by the presence of a neutral person, such as a facilitator, who can listen with a "third ear."

- **Learn to recognize and interpret emotions.** Earlier in this chapter we discussed the need for emotional intelligence: recognizing and understanding one's own emotions as well as those of others. Emotions provide signals of previous patterns and experiences. Learning what emotions indicate and their reliability improves one's ability to know when to count on intuition, and association leaders will need these skills to practice shared intuition.

- **Communicate.** The reasoning behind intuition must be explored fully through effective communication, discussion, and understanding. Failure to practice open communication may ultimately undermine the decision's acceptance and impact. Boards must establish a governance culture where open, honest communication is possible and practiced routinely. Because shared intuition requires a high level of trust, open communication among board members is essential. There can be no "hold-outs;" everyone must be on board to make effective decisions in this way.

- **Examine underlying assumptions.** In any given decision, underlying assumptions shared by the group or by individuals may be a factor. Shared intuition requires the identification of assumptions in a group, and a reasonable level of discussion to vet them. Are they based on reliable facts and evidence? Do patterns from the past suggest their viability? Boards need to discuss these in decision-making processes that use shared intuition. The ability for leaders to identify their individual assumptions about any given situation can have a direct impact on the degree to which they are able to accept change and to lead others through change. In Chapter 6, we discuss this further.

• **Use a shorter but structured process when time allows.** This process should provide a framework for capturing and learning from previous decisions and guard against errors that can occur when using intuition alone. Sometimes the informality that occurs with shared intuition can carry a risk that the decision-making process descends into almost informal conversation rather than formal deliberation. Using a short, focused discussion guide such as the dynamic decision-making process outlined in Chapter 3 will be of great value to boards in this area.

• **Increase experiences.** To learn and grow, leaders, boards, groups, and teams need to constantly try new things. Patterns of recognition develop from experiences. More experiences will create and shape successful patterns and lead to better intuition at both individual and group levels.

• **Create the right learning environment and culture.** Better intuitive decision-making comes from making more decisions, some of which may carry higher risk than others. An organizational culture with a high tolerance for risk and/or a high acceptance of mistakes enables individuals and groups to examine decisions without attacking the pride and dignity of the persons making them and leads to better intuitive choices.

Heightened intuition should not be used all the time for all decisions. It must be balanced with data and other input. But it holds great potential for individuals and groups to make better decisions in a more complex world.

Thoughts to Consider About Heightened Intuition

- What do I know about my own intuition?
- When do I hear it in my thought or decision-making process?
- When I am in the process of decision-making, do I know or listen to how I feel about the issue at hand?
- What do my instincts tell me about the issue at hand?
- How do my instincts affect how I perceive the issue at hand?
- What do I know about my emotional intelligence capacity?
- How can our organization's groups work to develop shared intuition?
- How can we keep our board out of "groupthink" or tunnel vision?
- How can I improve the intuitive mechanisms of my board or my organization?

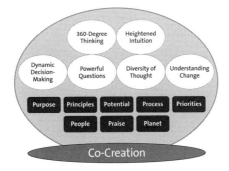

CHAPTER 3

Dynamic Decision-Making

THE TYPICAL BOARD AGENDA is changing. Associations have long been encouraged to practice data-driven or knowledge-based decision-making. In fact, many associations are drowning in data. The complexity of decisions and the quantity of decisions that leaders are being asked to make defies the ability of any individual or group of individuals to comprehend and process all the available information. And if we are honest, sometimes we don't have the time, resources, or budget to track down all the data necessary to arrive at a rational decision. And we know that many association boards have said that they will never have all the data necessary to make a decision. Additionally, board meetings are becoming shorter, board time is becoming scarcer, and board agendas are now full of complex strategic issues that require comprehension and synthesis of data, information, reflection, and thought.

The Case for a New Way to Make Decisions

Many organizations in the corporate sector have institutionalized data-driven decision-making by using a "rational decision-making approach." They have been influenced by the Nobel Prize-winning work of Herbert A. Simon, who originated the concept of bounded rationality in his *Models of Man, Social and Rational: Mathematical Essays on Rational Human Behavior in a Social Setting* (1957). Bounded rationality is the idea that in decision-making, the rationality of individuals is limited by the information they have, the cognitive limitations of their minds, and the finite amount of time they have to make a decision. It was proposed as an alternative basis for the mathematical model of decision-making. Bounded rationality aims at making optimal decisions based on careful evaluation of alternative courses of action and views the decision-making process as a sequential series of activities leading from an initial recognition of a problem, through the delineation and evaluation of alternative courses of action and the selection of the preferred alternative, to the implementation of action.

But Simon noted bounded rationality recognizes that it is impossible to comprehend and analyze all the potentially relevant information in making choices. The only possible way of coping with the complexity of the world is to develop techniques, habits, and standard operating procedures to facilitate decision-making. The point of bounded rationality is not that people might decide differently if they had more or different information. Rather it is that they can't process all the information even if they had it.

M. J. Church in *Intuition, Leadership, and Decision-Making: A Phenomenon* (2005), stated, "Today's fast-moving, high-tech, global workplace does not allow for lengthy deliberation and conventional, scientific management-like strategic approaches used to make decisions that require quick action." As we said in the last chapter, there has been a glamorization and mystification of leaders who are able to make decisions "from the gut" alone. Take, for example, Honda's entry into the U.S. motorcycle market, Ray Kroc's purchase of the McDonald's brand from the McDonald brothers, and Bob Lutz's decision to develop the Dodge Viper. In "Intuition in Strategic Decision-Making: Friend or Foe in the Fast-Paced 21st Century?"

Academy of Management Executive, 19(1), 2005, Miller and Ireland pointed out that many academic researchers, business writers, and managers "champion intuition as a key part of strategic decision-making effectiveness," and they predicted that "with success stories readily available, and with common sense suggesting intuition's necessity in times of change, intuitively dominated decisions are likely to increase in the fast-paced 21st century."

In the future, the ability of boards to comprehend vast data and make decisions in an effective and timely manner must take a quantum leap. What role should decision-making "from the gut" play in associations? Should association leaders continue to rely primarily on a data-driven approach? And considering the fact of having insufficient time for strategic conversations, how will boards reach consensus on increasingly complex issues?

Association leaders will increasingly need to rely on an appropriate and informed balance of data, intuition, and values. With heightened intuition identified as an essential leadership competency, there is a need for integrating intuition into organizational decision-making processes to enable associations to move beyond a data-driven approach. This chapter explores the manner in which intuition, balanced with data, can function in a flexible, dynamic decision-making model.

The Delicate Balance

The use of data and intuition is generally not an either-or proposition, and boards must incorporate dynamic flexibility in determining how much of each to use in any one decision. Patti Adye, in *Intuition and Leadership: The Art of Wise Decision-Making* (2004), states that decision-making becomes most effective when there is a better balance between intuitive and rational decision-making. "Developing intuition is not meant to eliminate the benefits of logical thinking; instead it is meant to bring forth a more holistic perspective to decision-making that embraces both the intuitive and the sensing dimensions of reality."

Shared intuition is often evident in the decision-making process when a group almost spontaneously has a sense of what the right path is and is in total agreement on it. Other times, however, a more careful data analysis is needed. And an overreliance on intuition can be as problematic as trying to rely solely on data. Therefore, a delicate balance is needed.

Moving forward, leaders and organizations will benefit from a decision-making model that balances data with a more intuitive focus, making the decision-making process more efficient. Increasingly, the complexity of associations and their environments will require leaders at all levels to rely more on intuition, values, and shared beliefs, and less on pure data to guide the decision-making process. The dynamic decision-making model enables leaders to more seamlessly move between data and intuition, between a quicker and a more deliberative pace.

Dynamic decision-making is when statistics meet senses. It's where research combines with gut reaction, where information blends with intuition, where facts support decisions that fit and feel right, based on an organization's purpose and principles. Dynamic decision-making blends facts and feelings. All leaders know that decisions must be rooted in fact. The most effective leaders also know that it is not simply an equation. It's not just about making the right decision; it's making the right decision for the right reason at the right time and involving the right people in the process. Dynamic decision-making ultimately yields greater commitment and follow-through to the decision and greater enfranchisement of members, stakeholders, and others affected by the decision because the passion and commitment of leaders becomes obvious—and infectious.

A Dynamic Decision-Making Model

Whenever a decision is made, an individual leader or a leadership team is really making a series of decisions about the decision. In the following diagram, we present the Dynamic Decision-Making Model, which not only provides a framework for blending intuition and data in the decision-making process but also explains how decisions are actually made from a cognitive standpoint.

Decisions are made in a multiphase process. When a leader (or group) becomes aware of the need for a decision, the leader (or group) is immediately confronted with a series of sub-decisions about how to make the decision. The sub-decisions constitute a

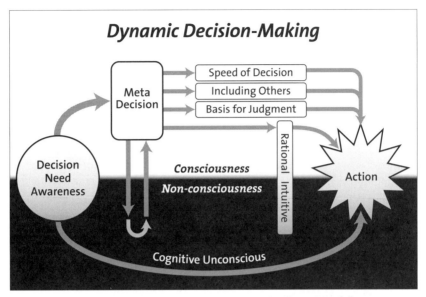

FIGURE 2. *A Dynamic Decision-Making Model*

meta-decision about the decision being made. The sub-decisions include

- How fast should the decision be made? (Should the decision be delayed?)
- Should other people be included or should the leader/group make the decision alone?
- What criteria, values, or standards will be used to make the decision?
- Can the decision be made using a purely intuitive focus, a purely rational one, or a hybrid of the styles?

An analysis of these meta-decisions surrounding a decision can serve as an important set of guidelines for an association board. In any key decision, a board should consider timing, additional stakeholder involvement, and values filters. If a decision is not time sensitive, the board may want to involve other stakeholders or take a careful look through the lenses of its shared principles.

The first three sub-decisions affect the fourth sub-decision about using an intuitive, rational, or blended decision-making approach.

If a decision has to be made very quickly, there may be no time to gather data needed for a rational approach. Boards may face this kind of situation when emerging issues have landed on their agenda, requiring action now, rather than at a future board meeting.

Dynamic decision-making has two important underlying assumptions: 1) The way we make decisions needs to change (be dynamic) based on the factors of the decision itself; and 2) Most leaders are prewired and predisposed to make decisions using an approach that they are comfortable with, and they need to be aware of their own tendencies and learn how to appropriately flex (to be dynamic) to fit the needs of each unique decision.

Interestingly, leaders (and groups) are typically prewired and predisposed in each of the components of the meta-decision. Some leaders like to make fast decisions. One corporate leader McNaught interviewed stated that he was predisposed to making quick decisions; he felt comfortable with fast decisions. But he said that from time to time, his boss would purposefully slow him down. He explained, "My boss has a saying that he's going to 'consult with the pillow.' That's his way of saying he's going to sleep on it."

Similarly, leaders are prewired for how inclusive they like to be in the decision-making process. Some leaders see themselves as the "Lone Ranger," while others see themselves as a cheerleader, encouraging others to come to consensus around a decision. Again, the needs and conditions of each decision and each association culture should dictate how inclusive the leader is in the decision-making process. If a particular decision demands buy-in from others and requires others to "own" the decision so that they will support it, a leader may need to alter his or her natural decision-making style and involve others in the process. Leaders must be flexible to accommodate the needs of each situation.

Ample research supports a need for a dynamic, flexible, holistic method of blending fact and intuition in decision-making. Sadler-Smith and Shefy, in "The Intuitive Executive: Understanding and Applying 'Gut Feel' in Decision-Making" (2004), assert that intuition and rational analysis are not in opposition to each other, that intuition and rational analysis are better conceived as two parallel systems of knowing. "The rational and the intuitive systems are not unbridgeable, and the challenge is to weave the two together and integrate intuition with rationality in order to make intelligent use of intuitive judgments."

Herbert Simon, in *Administrative Behaviour: A Study of Decision-Making Processes in Administrative Organizations* (1997), speculates that different situations may involve differing combinations of intuitive and rational decision-making. "More likely, there is a continuum of decision-making style involving an intimate combination of the two kinds of skill. We will likely also find that the nature of the problem to be solved will be a principal determinant of what mix will be most efficacious."

Sadler-Smith used the term *contextually appropriate* and says the ability to decide which decision-making mode to use is important. "As far as making decisions and solving problems in the real world is concerned, the vital skill is being able to judge when it's better to deploy analysis rather than intuition or vice versa." Figure 3 highlights the type of quantitative and qualitative information used in dynamic decision-making.

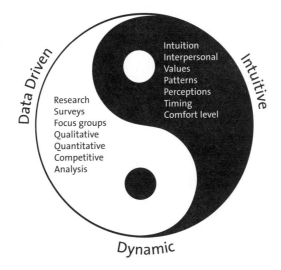

FIGURE 3. *Data and Intuition Sources*

Data-driven components—factors and sources such as research, surveys, focus groups, quantitative data, competitive analysis, financial analysis, and other data points—are depicted on the left side. On the right side, the less tangible, more intuitive elements include feedback from others through interpersonal relationships, timing, patterns, perceptions, principles, and values.

When It Makes Sense to Use Intuitive Decision-Making

Researchers Drury and Kitsopoulos, in "Do You Still Believe in the Seven Deadly Myths?" (*Consulting to Management,* March 2005), identify two of their seven deadly myths as "More Information Leads to Better Decisions," and "There Is No Problem That Can't Be Solved Rationally." Speaking on the latter, they agree with the idea that there are times when the rational decision-making process may not be the most rational approach. "When a group makes decisions, people's values, alternatives, and expectations interact, which makes it a less rational process. Yet this 'irrational' decision-making process often works best because it maximizes motivation and commitment."

We find that those leaders who have a preference for the "F" (feeling) on the MBTI, make decisions with emphasis on how people will be affected and on values. It seems possible for them to decide whether something is acceptable or agreeable without needing logical reasons.

In *Blink* (2005), Gladwell says that on straightforward choices, deliberate analysis is probably best, but "when we have to juggle many different variables, then our unconscious thought process may be superior."

We are not advocating for the abandonment of the data-driven approach. Relatively simple, straightforward decisions can and should be made predominantly with knowledge-based processes. However, we are finding that the more complex the issue is, the less straightforward the decision choices are and the more important it is to integrate intuition into the decision-making process. Sometimes, the addition of intuition can cut through the complexity of an issue and help a group come to timelier and more meaningful agreement.

When speed is critical to a successful outcome, expect to have to rely more heavily on intuitive decision-making. Choices made in battle or by first responders are informed by extensive training that helps build experience patterns that will improve intuition and decision-making. Boards often face critical decisions when a crisis erupts in the industry or profession they represent. For example, speedy responses are necessary when an association must make public statements about new legislation, accidents involving the deaths of leaders, or public scandals related to members.

Case Study of the Use of Dynamic Decision-Making

Building Owners and Managers of Georgia (BOMA-Georgia), a trade association serving commercial real estate professionals, was considering developing a new educational conference focused on environmental sustainability. First, the board evaluated whether developing such a program fit with its core purpose, principles (shared values), and existing priorities. This was the most significant item on the board meeting agenda and was the primary focus of the meeting. During the strategic conversation, board members and staff equally participated in the conversation and came to consensus that developing an environmental sustainability conference fit within the association's purpose and principles and that it was consistent with its existing priorities to educate its members and provide access to cutting-edge information.

Then the board chair and chief staff officer asked the following questions:

- What additional information to we need to make this decision?
- When do we want to make our final decision?
- Who will be responsible for making the final decision?
- What process will we follow to ensure the right decision is made, for the right reasons?

To make a final decision, the board decided it needed to research what competing programs already existed in the marketplace, its members' needs, and the association's capacity for developing such a program. The consensus was that the board would make a decision at its next meeting, which was in three months. Because of this tight timeline, the board delegated the responsibility for research to staff rather than to a committee or task force. To make the final decision, the board decided to allocate significant time on its next agenda to explore the data presented, decide whether to pursue the idea, and discuss options for program development if it decided to proceed. During the next three months, staff conducted extensive market analysis and member surveys and examined the impact on staff and member volunteers. In addition to this quantitative analysis, the chief staff officer and board members began bringing up the idea in conversations with members to gauge their responses. Leaders looked for patterns in the conversations.

The research revealed a significant number of environmental sustainability programs in the marketplace and a growing number of multiday conferences dedicated to this topic. However, the research also showed that very few educational programs were dedicated to the niche in which the association members operate and there were no multiday conferences. Furthermore, surveys revealed that members were highly interested in attending a conference if its sole focus were their niche within environmental sustainability. This quantitative data was supported by patterns identified in conversations with members. Both board members and staff began to realize that a conference focused specifically on their members needs related to environmental sustainability was needed and would be successful.

Finally, the staff conducted an internal review of the association's capacity to produce a new conference. This research included staff capacity, volunteer member capacity, and financial issues. In the previous fiscal year, the association had conducted a review of its major programs, and the board had decided to discontinue two of them. As a result, the association had the capacity to produce a new conference. The financial analysis showed support for the new initiative as well.

At the next meeting, the board chair and chief staff officer posed several questions to the board to spark conversation. The board didn't just analyze the data presented. They went further. They asked questions such as these:

- What are the data telling us?
- What patterns did we see in conversations with members?
- How do the data align with patterns we identified when talking with members?

When the board realized that the data were confirmed by their anecdotal evidence from talking with members, they formed a consensus that the association should move forward with program development. In making this decision, the board used both quantitative data and qualitative information—dynamic decision-making.

Intuition played an larger role in the decision about a date for the conference. Collectively, the board sensed that they had a limited timeframe in which to produce the niche event and be the first of its kind in the marketplace. A task force of members and staff was charged to plan, develop, market, and produce the program in six months.

Even though the timeframe was aggressive, staff and members met the challenge with enthusiasm because of the prospect of producing a first-of-its kind event for the industry. The association met and exceeded its goals. Not only was the conference launched on schedule, but it sold out. Since then, this annual conference has continued to exceed expectations in attendance, revenue, and, most importantly, creation of member value.

In dynamic decision-making, association leaders can use their knowledge of available data along with their own intuition, brain profiles, values, pattern recognition, and other intangibles to determine the right balance in any given decision.

Thoughts to Consider About Dynamic Decision-Making

- How do I make decisions as a leader today?
- What role does intuition play in my decisions?
- What role does data play?
- How do I balance the need for both?
- How does my association board make decisions today?
- What would the potential be for my organization to integrate intuition in our decision-making process?
- What would be the benefits?
- What would be the risks?

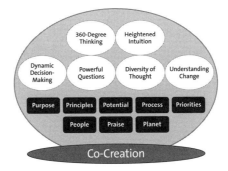

CHAPTER 4

Powerful Questions

NOWING WHAT QUESTIONS TO ask and when to ask them is a critical skill for association leaders. Asking questions—and actively listening to the answers—is something that is sometimes overlooked even by good leaders. Leaders sometimes feel pressured to have all the answers. Some leaders use simple, closed-ended questions and discourage lengthy dialogue. Unfortunately, associations face issues that cannot be addressed with simple questions and simple answers.

To be effective, association leaders must be aware of how they ask questions and how they listen to responses. Questions can be powerful if delivered correctly and inconsequential if asked poorly. Active listening adds to the information flow with more insightful perspectives that lead to better decisions and greater buy-in. Active listening and powerful questions allow otherwise taboo topics to be voiced, addressed, and resolved.

Powerful questions are open-ended, nondirective questions for which the asker does not seek predetermined answers. Furthermore, it is not simply the asking of such a question that makes it powerful. Leaders must also carefully listen and ask follow-up questions to clarify and truly understand responses to their questions. Laura Whitworth, Karen Kimsey-House, Henry Kimsey-House, and Phillip Sandahl , in *Co-Active Coaching* (2007), describe the attributes of a powerful question: "A powerful question evokes clarity, action, discovery, insight or commitment. It creates greater possibility, new learning, or clearer vision."

Asking powerful questions enables leaders to identify patterns in conversation and discussion. These patterns may reveal important information, such as new needs in the marketplace, important trends, and possible opportunities for the organization, which otherwise may be missed. Questions are powerful—and so are the patterns leaders see when they actively listen to the answers.

Michael J. Marquardt, in *Leading with Questions: How Leaders Find the Right Solutions By Knowing What To Ask* (2005), notes, "Astute leaders use questions to encourage full participation and teamwork, to spur innovation and outside-the-box thinking, to empower others, to build relationships with customers, to solve problems, and more. Recent research and the experience of a growing number of organizations now points to the conclusion that the most successful leaders lead with questions, and they use questions more frequently."

A question can be a powerful tool. Whether used to spur creativity or out-of-the-box thinking or just for solving a problem or evaluating an opportunity, a well-formed question makes us think. Asking powerful questions is an essential leadership competency. As Marquardt puts it, "Questions wake people up. They prompt new ideas. They show people new places, new ways of doing things. They help us admit that we don't know all the answers. They help us become more confident communicators."

Questions Create an Empowering Workplace
Marquardt notes, "Leaders who use questions effectively can truly empower people and change organizations." In associations, the power of asking questions is seen through the impact it has staff and volunteers. As one association executive explained, "In our

association, people have learned that it is OK to ask questions and that it is OK to share ideas, even those contrary to popular thought. This culture of asking questions has also enabled both staff and member leaders in our organization to better understand and deal with conflict."

It can be easy to shy away from asking questions. In fact, many people are not predisposed to ask them. This has shaped how many workplaces function. In some organizations, leaders often want instant answers rather more than more questions. Leaders often want to quickly strike items from their task list rather than ask questions that may lead to more work. These work environments may also cause leaders to ask closed- rather than open-ended questions. For example, in an agenda-packed meeting, when a board is trying to get through its agenda on time, the board chair may ask, "Any questions?" instead of, "What questions do you have?" The former moves the meeting along quickly, while the latter could significantly enhance the organization's success by encouraging more open dialogue.

Poorly asked questions can also demotivate others. For example, well-intentioned leaders may ask questions such as "What's the problem with this project? Why aren't we on schedule? Whose idea was that? Who messed up?" These questions intentionally or unintentionally cast blame; they may appear to the respondent to be disingenuous, attempting to trap them in an unfortunate answer. These are powerful but not necessarily productive questions.

Leaders should model the type of behavior they wish to see in others. In terms of asking questions, this means asking open-ended, genuine questions. The use of powerful questions encourages new ideas, open dialogue, and transparency and be can be an enormously powerful tool in modeling innovative, trusting, positive leadership.

Powerful Questions in Facilitation

Association leaders have long recognized the importance of facilitation skills, but how many leaders recognize that it is the use of powerful questions that makes facilitation effective? In fact, skill in using powerful questions is essential to successful facilitation.

Both staff and volunteer leaders can benefit from the very central and essential competency of learning to ask powerful questions while facilitating.

In *The Facilitator's Handbook* (1998), Fran Rees, notes, "Facilitation is a form of leadership...that helps to inspire, direct, and structure participation among people so that creativity, ownership, and productivity result." Good questions start with who, what, where, when, why, and how. Following are some examples of the types of questions that a good facilitator asks:

- What are you observing about...?
- Would you share with me what you are doing?
- What did you do and what happened?
- What is one thing you could do differently?
- How is this different from what has been tried before?
- What do you think you need to do for that to happen?
- What could be the next step?
- How is this larger, smaller, faster, slower?

Understanding the Power of a Question

An excellent resource to understand the power of questions is *Change Your Questions, Change Your Life: 10 Powerful Tools for Life and Work* (2004) by Marilee G. Adams. The book is written in the form of a parable about a leader named Ben Knight, who eventually achieves breakthroughs that save his career as well as his marriage. His success rests on having become a "question man" and an inquiring leader rather than a judgmental, know-it-all answer man. The book's central theme is that any of us can change our lives simply by changing the questions we ask, especially those we ask ourselves. We can ask questions that open us to learning, connection, satisfaction, and success. Or we can ask questions that impede progress and keep us from getting results we want. Asking, "What great things could happen today?" creates very different expectations, moods, and energy than asking, "What could go wrong today?"

In many board meetings, discussion is often superficial, with leaders asking questions to which the answers are predetermined.

Few boards allocate sufficient time on their agenda for the exploration of issues of strategic importance. Many questions are focused on gathering specific data, so that individuals are able to make data-driven decisions. Those questions are usually specific and focused, and many facilitate only narrow discussion of the issues.

Successful organizations tend to allocate more time to exploring strategic issues and facilitating a dialogue in which members and staff are equally encouraged to speak openly.

While many boards have effective ground rules that involve being respectful of each other's views, observing time boundaries, and ultimately agreeing to communicate the will of the group when talking externally about decisions that have been made, few boards have truly begun to understand the power of questions.

One board chair of a professional society that had experienced significant leadership challenges in recent years prided himself on leading very efficient meetings. With an agenda timed to the minute, he presided over information sharing and board decisions.

Some of the things that the board was asked to discuss were substantial, such as positions on industry issues and fundamental changes to the association's business lines and member services. The discussion led by this board chair consisted of information being shared, followed by, "Any questions?" In most cases, despite the breadth and depth of these issues, the answer was no.

Out of a nine-member board, five board members were in their first year, and the others held significant concerns about the association's slipping back into some of the leadership issues that had held the organization back in recent years. This board chair was running an efficient meeting, but he was not encouraging the open dialogue that was necessary for this board to fully understand and embrace the decisions the group needed to make.

What could this board chair have done differently? The message he unwittingly communicated in his approach was that questions were not welcome, and to the new board members, he was intimidating.

A board chair who understands the power of a question and is able to practice emotional intelligence by reading the discomfort on his board members faces, would have been able to stop and ask:

"What questions do you have about this material?" "Why is this an important topic for us?" "Whose views have we not considered in this decision that would be important for us to hear before moving forward?" "What would be the implications of our not acting on this issue?" "What does the timing of our circumstances now suggest about how quickly we need to act on this issue?" "What would happen to our membership and our industry if we failed to act on this issue?" "Are we really the right association to be addressing this particular industry issue? Is this really our mission?"

Powerful questions yield powerful dialogue and discussion. But it's not enough just to ask questions. The ground rules and operating agreements within the board or workgroup also need to support the dialogue that ensues from these questions. The culture of the group needs to support movement from basic questioning to these deeper, more powerful questions. In the same way that many boards have learned to move seamlessly from operational to strategic discussions, boards will need to develop the competency to move from basic objective questions into the deeper dialogue that powerful questions will yield.

A Framework for Four Kinds of Powerful Questions

There are many kinds of questions, and each yields different but essential dialogue. Terrence Maltbia, of the Columbia University Executive and Organizational Coaching Program, has created a model that supports the use of powerful questions. The model, known as the ORID (Objective, Reflective, Interpretive, Decisional) Framework for the first letter of each step, was designed primarily for use by executive coaches working in organizations to help individuals and groups unlock the issues that hold them back. This model, based on the work of Brian Stansfield in *The Art of Focused Conversation: 100 Ways to Access Group Wisdom in the Workplace* (2000), provides a framework for asking four kinds of questions:

• **Objective questions.** To bring facts to the surface, direct observable data, and generate a common pool of knowledge needed understand the context.

- **Reflective questions.** To explore feelings, emotions, and personal connections to the situation to help access gut level intuitive responses.

- **Interpretive questions.** To help make sense of the situation by examining related principles and values, underlying assumptions, significance of the big picture, and potential implications.

- **Decisional questions.** To help us move to action, to express commitments, to inform future action, and to move to closure.

Reflective questions are less commonly used by association leaders. Although leaders may talk about gut feelings related to particular decisions, they are rarely encouraged to explore feelings, emotions, or personal connections during meetings and decision-making processes. Concerns may arise when those emotions and feelings have a disproportionate impact on the dialog and tend to sway the discussion.

Obviously, a balance must be achieved. The best leaders use reflective questions to help people understand how emotions affect their perceptions of issues and best resolutions.

It is critical to good decision-making to establish a more meaningful, intuitive connection with the issue. Whether it is individual leaders beginning to understand and explore their own intuition in a particular decision a group beginning to explore the concept of shared intuition, reflective questions are essential to good dialog and decision-making.

Interpretive questions are useful in discovering the big picture and making sense of a situation. What trends are apparent? What has been established as fact, and what remains to be discovered? Successful organizations engage in a process of strategic planning that includes a review of the underlying assumptions on which the plan is built and a scan of changes to the environment in which the organization exists.

If association leaders were able to ask interpretive questions more often, it might help groups to see the larger picture and perhaps the underlying opportunities or threats inherent in a particular situation. And it would help individual association leaders and groups incorporate 360-degree thinking.

Finally, there are decisional questions. While many association leaders may believe that they excel in this competency, it is also the area in which there is the most room for growth.

After all the data have been collected, the inevitable question becomes what to do with it. Decisional questions help to move a group at the right time to the right next action. Sometimes, before they can take that next action, it is necessary for a board to ask simply, "What's next? What are the priorities?"

Association leaders who know how to pose decisional questions at the right time can help to facilitate closure, even if the final decision is not yet apparent. Decisional questions can help a group move forward from where they are to where they need to go next— to move a discussion forward toward conclusion.

The use of this framework and the ability for leaders to ask questions in each of these dimensions help to enrich dialogue, make decisions better, and sustain positive change.

The most effective leaders are adept at moving a group through these kinds of questions so that full exploration of an issue is possible and greater buy-in to the decision is the result. But using this framework requires an understanding by all involved and agreement to move to that deeper level of inquiry and dialogue, and reflective questions especially need to be used when people are comfortable and open and a trusting environment and relationship has already been built.

The use of powerful questions must be considered carefully by leaders. Using them incorrectly can produce unintended consequences. For example, consider a chief staff officer who, in a staff meeting during his first few months on the job, addressed a special agenda item called "teambuilding." He abruptly asked the staff, "If you had only 30 minutes left to live, what would you do in that time and how would you feel about it?" A powerful question to be sure and a reflective one but used with very poor timing!

As each staff member answered, the group slowly began to move from feeling vulnerable to feeling growing trust, but the feeling was quickly erased when the chief staff officer abruptly ended the conversation. "Great job on this teambuilding exercise," he said. "Now let's move to committee reports."

This abrupt change of direction confused staff and erased the trust that was beginning to build between him and his team. The question was powerful, but it was not handled properly. And timing is everything.

Asking Powerful Questions Requires Good Listening

In *Co-Active Coaching* (2007), Whitworth, Kimsey-House, and Sandahl identify three levels of listening:

The first level is *internal listening,* where the awareness is mostly on ourselves. We may be hearing what others are saying, but inside our heads, we're really thinking about our own reaction to what is being said. There is a monologue of self-talk going in our heads, and we do not really comprehend all the information being shared.

The second level is *focused listening,* where we are paying more attention to the person who is speaking. At this level, we begin to understand more about where he or she is coming from. Executive coaches use this level of listening to gain a deeper sense of the facts, emotions, and behaviors that their clients have around a particular issue. Practicing this level of listening, association leaders can absorb more information about the issue as well as about the speaker. Here leaders can sense emotion, opinion, point of view, and other attributes particular to who is sharing the information and can deepen their information base in the decision-making process.

The third level is *global listening,* where we are listening at a deeper, almost meta-level. Whitworth and his co-authors describe it as though you and the speaker are "at the center of the universe, receiving information from everywhere at once." This level includes both fact and emotion, both information and intuition. It includes virtually everything that can be observed in any given situation. The listener is not just hearing the information but is processing its meaning simultaneously and often almost unconsciously. It is at this level that leaders are able to access their intuition. Listening at this level allows you to observe what is not directly observable. It allows you to absorb information that you can't even articulate—you just know it is there. This level of listening is not as common, but it is essential to the practice of shared intuitive decision-making in groups and to asking powerful questions.

Asking Powerful Questions Takes Courage

Sometimes, it takes courage to ask a powerful question. Sometimes it takes courage to ask a question that may shed doubt on an already agreed-upon direction. It takes courage to add a new idea or piece of information or insight that wasn't previously considered.

The concept of leadership courage comes to mind when considering Enron and similar corporate scandals of the early 2000s that led to the Sarbanes-Oxley Act of 2002 and greater financial controls as well as when examining the more recent crises involving banks and other financial services companies. Were leaders in these companies aware of relevant information regarding their companies' situation? Were they cognizant of the implications of the information? Did any have the courage to ask the tough questions that would lead to potentially unpopular actions? It takes courage to ask powerful questions and even more to act on the responses to those questions.

Do association leaders have the courage to ask powerful, tough questions, questions that might cause unpopular reactions? What kind of culture would support asking tough questions? Could it be done in a way that is seen as enriching conversation and deepening insights, rather than making the person asking the question look like someone with an agenda to control the discussion?

Judy Gray, CAE, former executive director of the Florida Society of Association Executives and now president of Florida-based CEO on Call, reflects on the idea of managerial courage:

> Managerial courage means doing what is right for the organization when you know it's going to be crushingly hard to deal with the repercussions. As leaders, we must make hard decisions about personnel issues and about the direction of our organizations as the market and the economy changes. If we put off or avoid dealing with these situations, people up and down the line get confused and lose respect for us. So, managerial courage means tough decisions in tough times. We have to want to be respected more than we want to be accepted or liked. We have to do what's right

for the organization even though we dread the hard times that can follow the tough decisions. It's required daily, yet we get very little credit for exhibiting managerial courage.

As Michael J. Marquardt notes in *Leading with Questions: How Leaders Find the Right Solutions by Knowing What to Ask* (2005):

> History is replete with tales of dire consequences experienced by leaders who did not ask questions.... Historians who carefully examined the events and details behind the disasters of the Titanic, the Challenger, and the Bay of Pigs have determined a common thread—the inability or unwillingness of leaders to raise questions about their concerns. Some group members were fearful that they were the only one who had a particular concern (when, in fact, it was later discovered that many people in the group had similar concerns). Others felt that their question had already been answered in the minds of other group members, and if they asked the question, it would be considered a dumb question; and they would be put down as being stupid or not going along with the group. Because people did not ask questions, people lost lives when the Titanic sank, when the Challenger crashed, and when President Kennedy authorized a covert attack on the Bay of Pigs in Cuba.

And sometimes, the most courageous question to ask is, "What questions are we most afraid to ask?"

Asking Questions Enables Learning

Using powerful questions creates a rich environment for learning. Leaders who think they know all the answers or must provide all the answer, miss opportunities to help others learn and to see patterns. They fail to draw on multiple perspectives and build new insight. Many executives close off learning. In their day-to-day interactions with staff they usually either issue instructions or make judgments about the ideas or performance of others. By telling rather than asking, they are actually making their organizations less smart, less aligned, and less energized every day.

In *Leading with Questions* (2005), Marquardt quotes Donald Peterson, former CEO of Ford Motor Company: "Asking more of the right questions reduces the need to have all the answers."

In *Good to Great* (2001), Jim Collins describes a successful CEO who uses questions a powerful way. When the CEO first began turning a company around, he started with the realization that he did not know what to do next. He resisted the urge to walk in with answers and, instead, began with questions for both his top team and his board. At each step along the way, he would keep asking questions until he had a clear picture of reality and its implications. Collins says, "When he started the long traverse from near bankruptcy to stellar results, he began with a remarkable answer to the questions of where to take the company—I don't know.... He resisted the urge to walk in with 'the answer.' Instead, once he had the right people on the bus, he began not with answers, but with questions. 'He was a real spark,' said a board member. 'He had the ability to ask questions that were just marvelous. We had some wonderful debates in the board room.'"

The ability of association leaders to ask powerful questions is an essential emerging leadership competency. Leaders must use this competency to support organizational goals. They must ask: Do the actions of individuals fit our organization's principles? Do our activities fulfill our purpose? Are our priorities in line with our potential? Do we have the correct processes in place to achieve the desired outcomes? Do we understand the consequences of our actions in relation to our impact on the planet and our relative external communities? And will what the organization seeks to achieve create and sustain positive change for our members and stakeholders and all of those we serve?

Thoughts to Consider About Powerful Questions

- How do I typically ask questions?
- What questions do I ask? Are they phrased in a positive manner, or are they seeking to place blame?
- What patterns do I see in the answers to the questions I ask?
- How actively do I listen when others speak?
- How well do I prepare for a discussion by reviewing the data about an issue and preparing substantive, powerful questions to be used in group dialog?
- How does our board structure conversations to be open and engaging? Do we use questions to ensure full discussion and participation?
- Do we support the use of powerful questions and take the time to answer them?
- How and when can I ask one of the most powerful questions of all: "What questions are we most afraid to ask?"
- What can I do to create an organizational culture in which powerful questions are encouraged and appreciated?

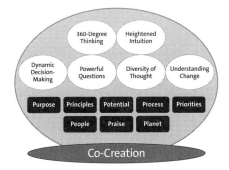

CHAPTER 5

Diversity of Thought

DIVERSITY OF THOUGHT ENABLES leaders to make better decisions by engaging new perspectives and creating greater buy-in and enfranchisement in leadership. It brings more voices into the decision-making process, a positive factor for associations that are struggling to function under aging governance structures and member connection mechanisms.

Diversity of thought means that individual leaders, at any given time, are open to diverse ideas, some of which may conflict with their own understanding or assumptions. Association leaders must abandon thinking as usual and ensure that they are open to ideas from a broad set of perspectives.

In the idea-rich environment in which association leaders will be operating in the future, it is essential that association leaders not fall prey to the trap of using the same ideas they have always used, drawing from the same sources they have always consulted, listening to the same people, harboring the same assumptions, and reaching the same conclusions.

Leaders who persist in looking straight ahead rather than taking a broader view of ideas and insight from all around them will not be successful. Producing an environment in which boards, committees, and other workgroups experience diversity of thought enables individuals to become better thinkers and better doers.

FIGURE 4. *Seeing Things Differently*

This illustration has been used by trainers, coaches, and psychologists for years, highlighting the interesting dynamic that different people see things in different perspectives. Depending on the perspective, one could see either a young lady or an old woman in the picture above. Which do you see? Both perceptions are equally correct and equally valid.

Diversity of thought means that an association leader has the ability to seek, explore, understand, appreciate, and respect multiple perspectives. Creating an association where individuals are free to express their differences and where individuals with different opinions can thrive, adds richness, perspective, and diversity of thought to the discussion of any issue. Randy Hain, managing partner of Bell Oaks Executive Search, Atlanta, writing in "The Diversity of Thought" (2007), gives us a perspective on diversity of thought:

> The term *diversity* is taking on new meaning among companies that are focused on building dedicated and strategic workforces.

Most sizable companies today utilize some form of diversity initiative in an effort to provide appropriate jobs and career opportunities for minorities and women. These initiatives typically address race and gender, but how often do companies' hiring policies target candidates who think differently and don't fit the traditional culture standard that has been in place since the company was founded? Diversity of thought—often the last form of diversity to seep into a company's culture—is becoming an important recruiting strategy for today's leading organizations.

Noting the need for diversity of thought, Hain suggests that it is essential that leaders listen to many different voices and quotes Jim Collins' *Good to Great* (2001):

Indeed, one of the crucial elements in taking a company from good to great is somewhat paradoxical. You need executives, on the one hand, who argue and debate—sometimes violently—in pursuit of the best answers; yet, on the other hand, you need those who unify behind a decision regardless of parochial interests.

Terrence E. Maltbia, program director of Columbia University's Coaching Certification Program, has written extensively about organizational diversity. In the book cowritten with Anne Power, *A Leader's Guide to Leveraging Diversity: Strategic Learning Capabilities for Breakthrough Performance* (2008), Maltbia notes, "It is important for leaders to be fully engaged during conversations. It is the combined force of head, hand, and heart work that promotes diversity's two guiding principles of 1) respect for the individual and 2) integrity through authentic leadership. To succeed at diversity, you must imbed these principles in your core values and demonstrate them in every human interaction occurring in your organization on a daily basis."

The Dimensions of Diversity
Maltbia has created a model (Figure 5) that illuminates diversity in a variety of dimensions, and we will explore how each dimension relates to the association environment because each has significant implications for enabling association leaders to understand diversity of thought as a competency. There are implications for

board composition, staff selection, and volunteer fit, among other possibilities.

Dimensions of Diversity of Thought

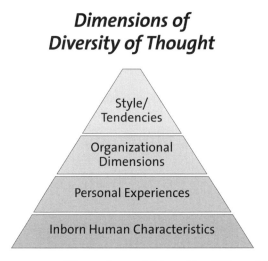

FIGURE 5. *Dimensions of Diversity of Thought*

Inborn Human Characteristics

The first level of diverse thought concerns inborn human characteristics. This often includes the demographic attributes of race, gender, ethnicity, country of origin, age, and sexual orientation, among others. Frequently, an association, through its nominations process, will seek to achieve an informal balance of these characteristics.

What are some of the dynamics that may be achieved in terms of diversity of thought when a board has a good mix of these inborn human characteristics? The potential is significant. For an association based in the United States or North America with aspirations of global growth, a culturally diverse viewpoint is essential to growth. For associations serving professions undergoing significant generational shifts, it is essential to have new voices at the table. For associations whose members are seeking to add greater diversity in the profession itself, it is advantageous to model that behavior in board selection. Too often, association governance is leading from behind in terms of being truly reflective of the demographics of the membership and the profession. Moving out in front of these issues and becoming a model for what the profession seeks to achieve would be an excellent strategy.

Generational Diversity

Another inborn human characteristic that carries great significance is generational difference. In *Passion and Purpose: Stories from the Best and Brightest Young Business Leaders* (2011), Coleman, Gulati, and Segovia note that the priorities of these young leaders are different: "For young leaders today, we believe the core issues are sector convergence, globalization, people leadership and diversity, educational evolution, technology, and sustainability. As labor force participation increases and old racial, class-based, religious, and gender barriers are gradually lowered, the workplace will benefit from the multiplicity of perspectives that these newly integrated groups can bring."

Clearly, generational diversity is a significant factor for associations as well as the professions or industries they serve. Most associations concurrently seek to serve multiple generations of active membership, and many have made great progress in bringing younger members on their boards. However, age alone does not guarantee diversity of thought. It is still possible to produce a group that is diverse in age but uniform in thought. Sometimes, younger members are hindered from making greater contributions because they sense that the association's structure and culture will not support their full participation.

Passion and Purpose suggests that younger leaders will be guided much more by their values than by traditional command-and-control management: "The return of the right brain is occurring at a time when employees—particularly Gen Y workers—are no longer enamored with their jobs but disgusted with the cynical, hypocritical, and obsessively left-brain management behaviors they see all around them in corporate life."

In associations, how will the cultural attributes of established governance systems, processes, and cultures differ with more traditional leadership values? We believe there are several areas of potential disconnects.

Participation. Traditional association values suggest that people are often selected for leadership based on their longevity and not necessarily on what they can contribute. In the value sets of emerging generations of leaders, everyone's contributions are valued equally, regardless of longevity.

Governance and control. Many association governance systems are still hierarchical and are controlled by long-serving volunteers. But in emerging generations of leaders, self-forming, peer-governed communities are the norm, and younger leaders may have less interest or patience in navigating through complex governance systems that require years of service before they can make a meaningful contribution.

Transparency. Associations often struggle with how much information to release and to what audiences at what times. In many associations, the perception of secrecy still exists, and mistrust among organizational components and constituencies is still rampant. Emerging generations of leaders see information as something to be shared, not controlled, and younger leaders may grow impatient and disenfranchised with what they perceive to be a lack of transparency in association communications.

Authenticity. In a May 4, 2009 post titled "The Power of Frustration" on the blog Get Me Jamie Notter, Washington DC-based consultant Jamie Notter raised significant questions about authenticity as an association cultural attribute, and we think it has relevance to generational issues.

> With the advent of social media, more things get said, and more ideas are shared, often without the traditional vetting and filters that associations have become used to, and in many cases, have played a gatekeeper role in providing control. But the barriers to communication have fallen dramatically. More people now say more things to wider and wider audiences. We expect and demand authenticity, so it's more "normal" for people to say just what is on their mind. That includes criticisms and frustration. But this will be a challenge to many organizational cultures.

Notter asks, "Does your association have the capacity to embrace frustration and criticism? Is your organization listening carefully enough to different parts of the system to pick up on frustration in time? If the points they were making were valid, would your organization actually be able to make changes, real-time?"

The answers to these questions lie to some extent in the ability of the association to be able to embrace diversity of thought. Diversity of thought allows multiple voices, questions, and ideas to surface, regardless of underlying organizational and industry or profession-related cultural assumptions. And one place where diversity of thought will have significance is an association's ability to embrace emerging generations of leaders who may not only expect new ways of interacting but if they do not perceive them, may disconnect from participation in the association altogether.

Gender

Gender is another type of inborn human characteristic. In many industries and professions, gender diversity is a challenge. In many organizations, boards may or may not reflect the demographics of their membership.

Many industries and professions have changed in regard to gender issues. Women are becoming dominant in many healthcare professions, for example, and are overtaking males in some professions. Some associations serving such professions, however, are still dominated by male leaders, using a traditional board structure that is not reflective of changes in the profession, in this case reflecting gender. Male association leaders may think they know what's best for the profession and the organization, but they are missing a female point of view that reflects, or may reflect, the future of the profession. In professions that are primarily female, getting the male perspectives is key.

Geographic and Cultural Diversity

Geographic location and culture are other important characteristics to consider in creating diversity of thought. Many boards seek to become "global in nature," to represent an emerging global membership, or to just appear "global." But very few boards have actually attained the level of sophistication from a cultural and a governance standpoint to actually be able to effectively use the talents of board members from other countries, whether they are expats in the United States or people residing in countries around the globe.

Understanding global cultures and preferences extends beyond basic demographics. Many association boards look at their membership populations and attempt, in good faith, to create positions on their board for members from countries and marketplaces where the profession is flourishing. But expanding board composition to include geographic diversity is not enough. Association leaders must also acquire deeper understanding of the cultural preferences and norms that individuals from other countries bring—how they perceive the world, how they approach work, how they make decisions, and how they lead. This will enable associations to truly become global, leverage diversity of thought, and fully maximize their global potential.

Geert Hofstede's work *Cultures and Organizations: The Software of the Mind* (1996) lays out a number of dynamics regarding cultural preferences and perspectives. ITAP International, a global training consulting company with U.S. offices in New Jersey, developed a leadership tool based on Hofstade's work called the "Culture in the Workplace Questionnaire." The CWQ (2011) measures individual leader capabilities to understand cultural dynamics and to work successfully with leaders from other cultures. The tool describes cultural attributes that extend far beyond country of origin, although it is normed in 150 different countries. Respondents gain a view of their cultural preferences through an online profile that is based on five dimensions: individualism, power distance, certainty, achievement, and time orientation:

- **Individualism** is the degree to which action is taken for the benefit of the individual or group.

- **Power distance** is the degree to which inequality or distance between those in charge and the less powerful subordinate is accepted.

- **Certainty** is the extent to which people prefer rules, regulations, and controls or are more comfortable with unstructured, ambiguous, or unpredictable situations.

- **Achievement** is the degree to which we focus on goal achievement and work or quality of life and caring for others.

- **Time orientation** is the extent to which members of a society are prepared to adapt to reach a desirable future or the extent to which they take their guidance from the past and focus on fulfilling their present needs and desires.

Hofstede's work has significant meaning for how association boards operate. Consider a board where there are many vocal American members. These individuals frequently and eloquently articulate their views and seek to sway the rest of the board to agreement with their positions. But members who are from places where the cultural norm demands that individuals subsume their own thoughts to the will of the group are far less likely to participate in board discussions or to perform their board functions in the same way. They may be reluctant to voice different perspectives in a discussion or put their names forward for officer positions.

Picture a board that is trying to make a decision. Some board members are from countries with a high tolerance for ambiguity, encouraging innovation and new ideas including out-of-the-box thinking and risk taking. Those members are likely to be comfortable with a higher degree of intuitive insight in the decision process. On that same board are people from cultures that demand certainty, and those board members have a greater comfort level in structured environments and a lower comfort level with intuitive thought and may, therefore, need a higher mix of data in the decision-making process.

Consider another example in which a board has a member who is from a culture where hierarchical orientation dictates that inequalities among people are expected and desired, power figures know all the answers, subordinates do as they are told without questioning others, and individuals do not suggest solutions for problems unless specifically asked. This board member, despite all the best intentions of the leadership team to create group norms that encourage open dialogue, is not likely to participate fully in group discussions. He or she would be more likely to wait for the board chair or other person in a perceived authority role to state their position and then support it without comment.

While the participative board members may encourage those with hierarchical orientation to be open, to speak their minds, and to comment in discussions, those with the hierarchical orientation are naturally predisposed to be uncomfortable in that role.

Many associations recruit directors from throughout the world but fail to have a clear understanding of the differences that these cultural dimensions can bring to board service. Failing to understand these cultural dynamics, many associations are unable to create an environment in which all board members are engaged and feel comfortable contributing in a meaningful way.

Diversity of thought can be achieved only when all board members are comfortable in a governance culture that supports their unique perspectives, points of view, and preferences. Organizations that seek to be successful in the competency of diversity of thought will need to ensure that there is a deeper level of understanding about the different preferences that people may have based on their cultural dynamics.

Personal Experiences
The nature of an individual's personal experiences is also a dimension that contributes to diversity of thought for an organization. These experiences may include educational background, family and personal income, marital or parental status, religious beliefs, occupation, and military service.

The values individuals hold are shaped by these experiences and can have a significant impact on their points of view. Many of these dimensions affect how a board member might view issues related to education levels in the profession, whether he or she supports part- or full-time practitioners in the profession, or other issues related to how the association views and seeks to shape the profession or industry it represents. All of these dimensions can collectively affect a board's decision-making. Associations that take these considerations into account can create the potential for rich dialog on many issues that will truly allow for greater diversity of thought.

Organizational Dimensions

The next level of the diverse-thought model is organizational dimensions. The term *organizational* here refers not to the association itself but to the function or role in which members work or, in the case of associations, the segment of the industry or profession in which they practice or work.

In a corporate environment, there may be different points of view among line-versus-staff management functions. Human resources people may see things differently from sales and marketing, finance differently from engineering, and so forth. This functionally centric kind of thinking is fairly typical in corporations, where corporate change efforts and other large-scale projects benefit from the inclusion of employees at various levels and across various functions within an organization in to gain a broad set of perspectives.

In an association, diversity related to organizational or industry dimensions takes on a slightly different dynamic. Most associations seek to populate leadership with members who hold a variety of positions within their profession or industry. Bringing together these individuals can make for a rich, diverse dialogue, and many associations succeed in populating boards, task forces, and other volunteer entities with diverse representation of the membership.

Organizational diversity can also be magnified by leveraging the unique dynamics of a profession. Many associations serve industries, professions, or causes that are multidisciplinary. They may bring together members, stakeholders, and donors from a variety of professions, and the common interest area is something other than the individual's primary employment.

Think, for example, of a certification board within a healthcare sector, whose membership represents many different professions. Each individual profession carries its own point of view, its own values, and its own culture. Nurses, physicians, mid-level practitioners, allied professionals, and the public—all may have an interest and involvement in a particular organization. In successful organizations, groups that are created have the potential to yield many different views, cultures, and priorities.

Many associations have made progress in composing groups with diverse perspectives. Good work has been done on understanding membership status, needs, wants, expectations, and priorities, and that information has been effectively leveraged in board composition, volunteer task force or committee makeup, and research populations for projects seeking input on issues affecting the profession.

While there has been much progress on the volunteer side, what associations may need to focus on more effectively is representing these diverse points of view in the staff. Staff is often called on not just to provide data but also to provide insight and perspective that informs the volunteer leadership's decision-making processes. Collaboration between volunteer members and professional staff enables organizations to make well-informed decisions, using diversity of thought and resulting in true volunteer-staff partnership. The blending of perspectives among industry professionals and association management specialists creates a balance of vision, strategy, and execution and plays a role in educating and informing staff about the dynamics of the profession. A good mix of industry or profession perspectives and professional association management perspectives makes a well-informed group that will be better equipped to achieve diversity of thought while coming to consensus on the most important issues.

Style and Tendencies

The final dimension of diversity in thought is the unique style and tendencies of individuals. These tendencies and styles include learning style, conflict-resolution style, problem-solving style, decision-making style, and responses to differences.

To better understand diversity among its members, corporate work teams routinely use basic assessment instruments such as the Myers-Briggs Type Indicator (MBTI) or Dominance, Influence Steadiness, Conscientiousness Indicator (DISC), or the Thomas Kilman Conflict Resolution Inventory. In many cases, these instruments are used in associations to create greater understanding and communication among volunteer leadership and staff by acknowledging individual communication, and conflict-resolution styles and other preferences.

We are aware of a number of association boards that have used instruments like these in board development activities, but we fear that they may not be used in a manner that yields their full potential, to understand and leverage differences in groups. They may just be used as a one-time exercise in an annual board development activity, and the full exploration of leveraging strengths and working through differences may not always be in focus. Granted, one of the challenges that many association boards face is extremely limited time together either because of fewer scheduled board meetings or rolling terms that result in constant changes in group composition.

But of greater concern is that in many board cultures, there is still an active debate over whether it is acceptable to actually disagree! In an earlier chapter we referenced the concept of a straw poll "thumbs" pre-decision-making mechanism. The problem that some groups encounter in using this method is that it may encourage a drive to create conformity in the interest of achieving consensus more quickly. In other words, an unconscious cultural norm emerges, causing people to think that the objective of the group's process is to have everyone in total agreement.

In fact, many boards do not know how to deal with conflict. This is an essential conversation in terms of encouraging diverse thought. For association leaders to be able to use the competency of diversity of thought, they will need to be comfortable with conflict. They will need to be able to encourage a decision and dialogue process separating individuals from their views so that disagreements are over issues, not conflicts between individuals. Associations by nature are collaborative, warm, collegial communities, and people basically hate to disagree. When a decision or dialogue is framed in the way that disagreeing with a point of view translates immediately to disliking a person, conflict occurs and diversity of thought is in jeopardy.

Association leaders also need to understand the impact of individual thinking preferences on their organizations. As is highlighted in the previous section, many organizations use

Myers-Briggs, DISC, and other assessments to improve communication, but few have used these tools to assist leaders in better understanding their thinking preferences. On a deeper level, tools that assess thinking preferences can be used to enable leaders to employ whole-brain thinking, which we explored in greater detail earlier in this text.

In the corporate sector, many people are hired for their technical competencies and then promoted into management and leadership positions without training about how to work with people and how to think holistically. The current view is that a leader's natural preference for left- or right-brain thinking is less important than his or her ability to be flexible in thinking preferences. Sometimes one or the other is more dominant or necessary, and the best leaders are becoming "whole-brain'" thinkers, as we referenced in Chapter 1.

Individual members of association boards can be better equipped to embrace diversity of thought, practice 360-degree thinking, and make better decisions through the use of tools that empower leaders to achieve greater self-knowledge.

The benefits of considering whole-brain thinking as a factor in creating diversity of thought are significant. Krister Lowe, partner in the New York-based C. Global Consulting, LLC, states, "Many people are hired for their technical competencies and then promoted into management/leadership positions without training on how to work with people and how to think holistically. A leader's natural preference for left- or right-brain thinking is not important; it is the ability to be flexible in thinking preferences that is critical." Lowe's firm works with large, international non-governmental organizations, and several leaders he is currently working with are inspiring their organizations to be more creative and innovative by using whole-brain thinking. Lowe asserts that the right-brain skills that built the organization are not enough moving forward; Future growth will depend on the blend of left- and right-brain thinking.

In Chapter 2, we shared the story of the Association of Pet Dog Trainers board's use of shared intuition. The APDT board's achievements were aided in part through team development using the Needling Brain Instrument (NBI) inventory (see Chapter 1). The inventory assisted the board in understanding their individual and group thinking preferences. Understanding if its members were right-brain, left-brain, intuitive, analytical, detail oriented, or big-picture thinkers enabled them to more effectively communicate, share that information, and make effective decisions. The impact of thinking preferences on the composition of association boards could be significant. Boards need whole-brain thinkers, but not everybody has strength in every area. Right-brained thinkers have strength in the dimension that yields strategic, big-picture ideas. Left-brained thinkers have the ability to put plans together to move ahead, and often have a more detail-oriented approach and are excellent in execution. Right-brain thinking may yield visionaries—people who are able to create a compelling sense of where to go and why we need to go there. Right-brain thinkers may be excellent communicators because of their empathy and sociability, and these are the individuals who will be excellent ambassadors to the membership, stakeholders, and others in the industry or profession they seek to influence.

Wouldn't it be excellent to be able to have this knowledge and insight during the nominations process, to have nominations committees that focus not just on the typical components and elements of experience that is needed but on the kinds of thinkers that the organization needs at any given time for its board?

One association was coming out of a difficult, multiyear period that was characterized by animosity, emotion, and backward momentum. In the first year with a new direction, inspired in part by a new board and a new CEO, the board engaged in a whole-brain thinking assessment as part of its board orientation, and members were able to compare individual results with a group composite. What they discovered was that each of them individually had distinct strengths: one in strategic thinking, several in execution, and others as strategic visionaries. But what they also learned in the group composite was that none of them had significant strength in empathy and communication. So they discovered that their weak point as a board was in communication and outreach, and this came at a time in the association's history when the membership already felt disenfranchised and distrustful of its leadership.

This scenario suggests is that while diversity of thought can be achieved through seeking whole-brain thinkers individually or amassing a team that has collective strength in both right- and left-brain skills, what is also important is looking at where the association is in terms of its evolution and history.

At some points, an association needs enfranchisers, ambassadors, and excellent communicators who can reach out to a membership that is disjointed or disinterested. At other times, an association needs leaders who are big-picture thinkers and can imagine and communicate a better tomorrow for the membership and the association. And at still other times, an association needs leaders who have a strategic focus to be able to put a plan together and guide its successful execution. Matching the right member leader to the right strategy needed at the right time is an excellent goal for associations.

For association leaders to achieve true diversity of thought, they must be aware of the dimensions of diversity of thought during the nominations and/or hiring processes, and have a commitment to leverage them as the team grows together.

Board Composition and Diversity of Thought

A frequent challenge when assembling a board or committee is that the most talented people do not automatically find roles in which they can best serve. It is a challenge for the association leader to find the balance between what volunteers think they do well, what they actually do well, and what the association needs them to do.

In some associations, the most valuable thinkers may remain unengaged because they are not naturally inclined to volunteer or they are not encouraged to pursue leadership roles. Often, the best, most diverse, and most valuable thinkers may go unused because their personality styles do not encourage them to volunteer for leadership positions.

Their cultural orientations may not encourage them to think that they are ready to climb the hierarchy, or they are comfortable working as individuals, preferring to be in the background as part of a working group and not having to shoulder the visibility of being an active leader.

Association boards are in the midst of an evolution. Many boards have moved beyond composition from a constituency basis (geographic or membership segment-specific slotted representation). Many have recognized that there is a need for competency-based boards (skills, knowledge-based) and have shifted in that direction. Successful associations will also need conscientious boards with the ability to see things holistically and to balance data, intuition, experience, and insight from diverse points of view.

Constituency Based → **Competency Based** → **Conscientiously Based**

FIGURE 6. *Continuum of Board Composition*

Diversity of thought in all these dimensions holds great potential for improving board composition. But what about the organization whose leaders do not have the flexibility of changing the board structure or even the nominating process to any great extent? What kind of courage does it take to for leaders or associations to seek diverse thought? What can be said about an organization whose leaders choose to neutralize potential conflict by limiting discussion, negotiating positions behind the scenes, and bringing to the board a virtually finished decision ready for rubber-stamping? What risks are inherent in this strategy? In the contentious environments in which many associations are operating, there is a perceived risk in going into a board discussion without a predetermined outcome. This may make for smoother decisions and faster meetings, but we doubt that it makes for better decisions or greater buy-in in the long run.

The ability of the leaders of an organization to encourage diversity of thought is an essential competency for the future. The power of diversity of thought stems not only from establishing a board with the right people but also from creating opportunities for board member perspectives to be heard in a more meaningful way and encouraging input of all parties on all levels.

Thoughts to Consider About Diversity of Thought

- How does our board engage in dialogue that reflects diverse thought?

- How does our board of directors respond to ideas that are "out of the mainstream"?

- How does our board of directors encourage disagreement in dialogue?

- How do we ensure we examine an issue from multiple perspectives?

- How does our leadership culture appeal to members who have a variety of thinking styles?

- How do we ensure our organization's leadership has diverse perspectives?

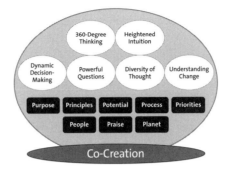

CHAPTER 6

Understanding Change

S OME LEADERS RESIST CHANGE, others gravitate toward it. Those who resist may do so because they lack understanding or knowledge of the sentiments and processes necessary to make it happen successfully. The key is to ensure a comfort level with change through open and continuous dialogue so that whatever change has been achieved will be sustained over time. Changing leadership on boards makes it difficult to sustain meaningful change unless the true drivers of change are accepted and understood.

What do association leaders need to understand about the nature of change? How does change happen within organizations, and how can association leaders help to identify and remove barriers to change in individual members, leaders, and stakeholders?

Change is constant, so constant, in fact, that leaders often complain of "change fatigue" in their organizations. While change itself may never be totally understood, new research enables leaders to better understand how to manage and lead change.

In most instances of organizational change, there are champions, followers, and opponents. Champions can see the ultimate realization of the envisioned change, what will happen as a result of the change, and how the organization may differ because of change. Followers believe that the champions know what they are doing, and so do not see the need to become involved with influencing the outcome. And opponents see something that they will lose, and they actively oppose change.

Every organization includes each of these dynamics, and it is the responsibility of leaders to facilitate change in a way that removes barriers and transforms opponents into champions. How do leaders do this? They understand the fundamental, underlying individual dynamics surrounding the acceptance of change.

Underlying Factors Affecting Change

Successful leaders know what actually contributes to change and what deters change in the minds of the people, including their own minds. Many competent managers do not understand the people element that drives or inhibits change.

In his book *The Practice of Adaptive Leadership: Tools and Tactics for Changing Your Organization and the World* (2009), Ronald Heifetz and his coauthors describe two distinct types of challenges that leaders face in driving change in organizations: technical and adaptive.

Technical challenges are problems that can be clearly defined and often addressed with known solutions, skills, and behaviors. Organizations leverage existing structures and procedures to address these challenges. As a result, no real change is required. It is often more a matter of training or adaptation of existing solutions and procedures.

Adaptive challenges are far more complex. They represent forces requiring significant shifts in individual habits, status, role, identity, or way of thinking. As a result, organizational leaders who initiate substantial change must help people to make these shifts.

The single biggest failure of leadership, in Heifetz's view, is to treat adaptive challenges like technical problems. Most leaders—both association executives and volunteer leaders—progress through organizational ranks primarily on the strength of their professional or technical knowledge. Their skill set and experience is built around solving technical challenges through analysis, logic, and experience. A technical challenge in an association might be the transition to a new member database. The technical mechanisms of migrating data can come from known skills and solutions. But the change in behavior required for members to input changes to their own membership records into a new database system is an adaptive challenge, and the leader's role in addressing that aspect is to encourage members to use the same coping mechanisms they used to make similar shifts in the past. Leaders must empathize, educate, illuminate, and reinforce progress.

Many leaders are not adept at dealing with adaptive challenges. The response pattern of technical leadership does not work well on adaptive challenges because these challenges are more about people's underlying hopes, fears, and expectations. These issues tend to arise in more significant change efforts that affect people's sense of identity, sense of purpose, or sense of power. While changes to an association's governance or committee structure may seem like technical challenges in terms of design and composition, any association leader knows that there is an adaptive aspect to that kind of change, and leaders need to open communication and demonstrate understanding in helping people deal with their reactions to these changes. A smaller board may make members feel disenfranchised because representation in governance may be structurally reduced or eliminated. A change in branding or association name may make people fear a loss of professional identity. In these cases, adaptive leadership skills have the potential to motivate people through deep-rooted and unexpressed needs, fears, priorities, and perspectives and to move them successfully toward new and productive ways of working, thinking, and changing.

How do leaders determine if the change requires a technical or an adaptive response? Heifetz and his colleagues indicate that adaptive challenges trigger an emotional response in those concerned. For example, if an association has implemented a change that results in a high number of complaints, this is an indication that the association is facing an adaptive challenge, even though there may be elements of a technical challenge present (such as a routine database conversion). If the database conversion goes poorly, and additional consultants are brought in to interview users and program more changes and if members and staff continue to express frustration and anger, the technical challenges are superseded by the adaptive element. No amount of extra programming will satisfy the fears and concerns of the users. The situation has already moved from technical to adaptive, and yet many association leaders in such a situation may choose to focus on the database itself rather than users' reactions to it. Adaptive challenges are often represented in situations that appear to persist or reappear following a short-term fix. Adaptive challenges can also be present if current beliefs, values, and assumptions of an organization or long-held values or truths seem to be getting in the way of progress.

Adaptive challenges require shifts in behavior. They require leaders to learn new skills, take on new roles, adopt new beliefs, and embrace values not previously considered. In the face of unprecedented challenges, many associations are forced to realign, downsize, reorganize, and reframe what sort of work is being done and by whom. Shifts in this area can be difficult because those who were comfortable with established skill sets may draw their identity from what they have always done. Conflict between stakeholders and groups is inherent in the change process. Such conflicts must be confronted, mediated, and resolved.

Overcoming Immunity to Change

Robert Kegan, who teaches in the Harvard University Graduate School of Education, and Lisa Laskow Lahey, the associate director of Harvard's Change Leadership Group, address how people react to change in their book *Immunity to Change: How to Overcome It and Unlock the Potential in Yourself and Your Organization* (2009). They build on the concepts of adaptive and technical challenges and explore how individuals and organizations often get in the way of their own change efforts.

Leaders sometimes initiate change by developing work plans and tasks lists that aim to alter behavior. Many times leaders fail because they do not understand the emotional factors that influence how individuals respond to change. These factors, including underlying fears and assumptions, are barriers that affect an individual's ability to accept change.

In *Immunity to Change,* Keegan and Lahey outline a process that enables leaders to identify clear, specific goals and to understand what actions the leader may be taking that reduce their likelihood of achieving success. They call this process "building an immunity map." The questions used include: "What is my goal (or change I am seeking to institute)? What would I need to do differently? What behaviors do I exhibit that go against my goal? What hidden competing commitments or worries are taking me away from my goal? What assumptions do I have that impact this change?"

The immunity map helps leaders better understand their hidden competing commitments and provides them with tools to test those beliefs. The results help leaders develop methods to modify their own behavior to achieve their goals and help them help others to do the same.

This approach can be a very powerful personal and professional leadership tool. Adaptive leaders are acutely aware of what they are thinking and how they are feeling, both positively and negatively, and how that may affect their behavior or response to change. Adaptive leaders are courageous leaders. They have a deep understanding of themselves and are able to better help others to understand and embrace change.

The Role of Coaching in Readying People for Change

Associations are service-based organizations that rely largely on developing and maximizing human capital and encouraging and motivating people to achieve organizational performance. Frequently, staff are hired for their technical competencies and subsequently promoted to positions of leadership without formal training about how to maximize human capital. Volunteer leaders are appointed or elected because of their professional or industry achievements, not necessarily for their leadership or motivational skills.

In May 2011, the Institute of Leadership & Management, a London-based management consultancy, issued a research report titled "Creating a Coaching Culture." Among their findings are that executive and organizational coaching is a particularly powerful tool that should be considered and used more extensively to develop individual and organizational performance and unlock human capability in associations. At its most powerful, coaching can deliver considerable benefits, help managers get the most from their teams and leaders get the most from volunteers, and boost engagement in workplaces of all types.

Specifically, coaching creates an environment in which people are more open to change. Coaching enables people to see opportunities within their organizations more clearly, to create a solid vision of the future, to define what they wish to accomplish individually and organizationally, and to identify how to overcome barriers to success.

Many organizations find it best to hire external coaches to work with leaders, executives, and managers. The role of an external coach is to help an individual identify personal or organizational goals, gather performance feedback, identify barriers to change, help people move to action, and hold them accountable for results. Associations are increasingly using executive coaches to

- Work with new chief staff officers to help maximize the association's investment in the new hire.

- Work with high-potential staff to help them develop leadership skills and advance into new positions.

- Work with board chairs and chief elected officers to help maximize their leadership competencies and gain new ones.

- Work with leadership teams of chief staff and chief elected officers to gain a greater understanding of working and thinking preferences and to negotiate more effective working relationships.

- Work with staff or volunteer leaders who have potential but have behaviors that are blocking their advancement.

• Work with boards in a deeper developmental role, helping them
  gain greater understanding of each other and build competencies
  such as shared intuition.

While much of this work can be accomplished with external
coaches, coaching is also increasingly being viewed as an essential
leadership skill, and internal organizational competency in coaching
is being developed in associations, governments, and the corporate
sector. Organizations are increasingly training staff management
in coaching skills for use in their own functional areas and in
other working opportunities, such as working with volunteers on
committees and task forces.

Coaching as a management competency helps to answer the
questions: Who is the person in front of me? What motivates this
person? What is he or she really thinking, feeling, and knowing?
Who are the people on this room? What do we do well individually
and as a team? What do we believe? What motivates us?

Many large corporations are beginning to integrate coaching into
their overall human capital strategy, and this is important for associations to consider as well. Because organizational success includes
developing and maximizing human capital, coaching is an important
component of the people foundation we discuss elsewhere in
this text.

Coaching provides many benefits for organizations, such
as: improved communication, transparency, more candid and
honest feedback, and improved performance management and
accountability.

Coaching also contributes to a culture that supports 360-degree
thinking and asking powerful questions. It engages people in
thought. It prepares people for change by helping them gain greater
understanding of their values, beliefs, assumptions, and concerns
and greater insight into how they affect behavior and action in the
organization they serve. Coaching also helps people trust their
intuition. Ultimately, coaching creates a climate of holistic leadership
competency.

The Role of Leadership

Who exactly in an association has the responsibility to support and maintain a focus toward change? Is it the volunteer leader whose tenure may be short? Is it the chief staff officer who maintains organizational memory and manages resources consistently over a period of years? What are the roles of volunteer and staff leadership in sustaining long-term culture change? How are champions for change created? Should every association have change champions or encourage their development?

In many associations, the role of change champion is played by a volunteer leader, and given the changing nature of the leadership of most associations, that fact poses a challenge. It is rare for an association to sustain its strategy and vision over time and even rarer that any two consecutive leaders see the path to that vision the same way. Change often lasts only as long as the leaders who wish to sustain it. If the case cannot be made for change over successive years and generations of leadership, the organization will not be able to realize its ultimate goals.

A change champion who is in a stable, long-term, and empowered position can transcend leadership changes and help maintain the focus of the organization toward achieving lasting change. In many associations, volunteer leaders change annually, and the professional staff is not often sufficiently empowered to lead decisively.

But in some associations, the chief staff officer, the individual who leads the organization long-term, is encouraged to be the champion of change. Expectations of member leaders in many associations suggest that more and more is being asked and expected of staff leadership, so staff must begin to see this as a potential role for themselves and part of their jobs in many cases.

In the end, it matters far less who fills the role of change champion than it does to decide to initiate change in the first place. Change champions will best be able to drive and sustain change if they truly understand the nature of how people react to it and whether the challenges are technical or adaptive. If they have identified potential barriers and how to overcome them, they will succeed in leading change.

In the end, associations must create organizational cultures that support and sustain the possibility of change. What is rewarded, what is valued, and what actually works must reflect principles of continuous creativity, and continuous improvement—looking for new ways to do things. The best ideas can sit in the minds of the best leaders, but if the organization they are operating in does not support change, nothing new will be accomplished.

The undeniable truth remains: Change is inevitable and organizations must keep moving forward. The association leader must be successful in enabling and embracing change. As everything is interconnected in an organizational ecosystem, a leader must be constantly aware of how a change in one area will affect not just each individual and component of the organization but also the organization as a whole. It is in the mastering of this holistic approach to management where the basic skills of leadership truly become an art.

While an organization can initiate the transition to a new system of governance or another change in culture, what does it really take to sustain change? If the energy and the vision reside only with leaders of change, broader enfranchisement among stakeholders will not be achieved, increasing the likelihood that future leaders will not continue implementation of the change and the effort will fail. Despite the seemingly logical, rational, and productive reasons for the change in any organization, association leaders must understand what causes people to accept or reject change.

Thoughts to Consider About Understanding Change

- What kinds of change have I as an individual leader been asked to lead?
- What do I know about the nature of resistance to those changes?
- What do I understand about helping people and organizations identify the barriers to change?
- How can I gain a better understanding of my own barriers to change?
- What role could coaching play in my organization to help break down the barriers to change?

PART II

Eight Essential Organizational Foundations

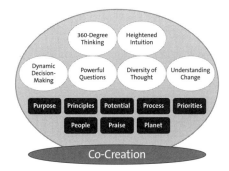

CHAPTER 7

Eight Essential Organizational Foundations— An Overview

F OR ASSOCIATION LEADERS TO take full advantage of the emerging leadership competencies of 360-degree thinking, heightened intuition, dynamic decision-making, powerful questions, diversity of thought, and understanding change, their organizations need to be balanced, holistic systems, in which creative thinking, dialogue, risk taking, diversity, open-mindedness, and, above all, people are valued.

New competencies can be exercised only in organizational environments that support them, and the organizational foundations we will describe here concern the systems, structures, and processes that should be in place to form a foundation for the practice this new thinking. We will explore eight essential organizational foundations in this chapter:

- **Purpose** is the reason for an organization's existence and, despite changes to the external environment or profession or issue areas in which the organization operates, purpose represents the one thing that members and stakeholders can never envision changing.

- **Principles** are beliefs and values that guide organization's behavior, decisions, and actions.

- **Potential** is a clear articulation of the future the organization wishes to create. Achievement of the organization's full potential is often expressed in its vision, goals, and aspirational statements. As organizations dedicate themselves to reaching their full potential, they can create positive change in the world.

- **Processes** are repeatable methods of executing work and making decisions. Leaders function best in organizations that have built processes that result in operational efficiencies and quality outcomes.

- **Priorities** represent a focused set of initiatives chosen in an operational time frame. Successful organizations select these priorities in light of their purpose and principles, while keeping in mind their limited resources of people, time, and money. Priorities are not about rank-ordering a long list; they are about selecting what to do and what not to do.

- **People** relationships in an organization should be based on mutual respect and trust, a shared understanding of the roles people play in organizational success. In an association, this includes staff, members, volunteers, and stakeholders; in other organizations, it may be employees and customers or clients, as appropriate to the organization's particular business model.

- **Praise** represents a genuine, expressed appreciation for the people within an organization as well as individuals served by it. Praise is about celebrating success and valuing the role that people play in achieving success.

- **Planet** is a clear understanding of how fulfilling purpose achieves positive change in the world around the organization. It means different things for different organizations and should not be confused with environmental sustainability. It is a fundamental awareness that what people and organizations do can have a ripple effect in the communities in which they operate and in the world as a whole.

While taken separately, none of these foundations are revolutionary. Each represents a separate area of focus, many of which have been established successfully in associations over time.

But what is critically important is that we now believe they are all essential and that they are all interconnected. We encourage the awareness of the interconnectedness of these foundations as elements in an organizational ecosystem.

How do these foundations interact like elements in an ecosystem? First, let's take a look at elements in an ecosystem in nature and how they interact. Similar to the Chinese theory of yin-yang, the theory of five elements—wood, fire, earth, metal and water—was an ancient philosophical concept used to explain the composition and phenomena of the physical universe.

A 2008 entry on the blog "Traditional Chinese Medicine Basics" (www.tcmbasics.com) notes that in traditional Chinese medicine, the theory of five elements is used to interpret the relationship between the physiology and pathology of the human body and the natural environment. According to the theory, the five elements constantly move and change, and the interdependence and mutual restraint of the five elements explain the complex connection between material objects as well as the unity between the human body and the natural world. The concept of mutual restraint refers to the idea that each element, although in constant movement, is aware of the other elements and will naturally create a balance through the act of restraining from motion or action. Organizationally, it suggests that good judgment is used whenever there is a perceived need and reason to hold back on one area to focus on another.

The organizational foundations as elements are also in constant movement, and the the complex connections among them suggests that the most successful organizations will not only recognize the interdependences but achieve a balance among them.

For example, if resources and priorities are directed toward potential, there is balance. If purpose and principles support shared leadership, there is balance. If praise and planet support the enfranchisement of people, there is balance. In other words, leaders practicing understanding their organizations as ecosystems understand the interrelationships of each of the organizational foundations and create harmony among them.

These foundations, while all important separately, also interact in a nonlinear, interconnected way. Changes made in one area often will have impact, intended or unintended, elsewhere throughout the system, and leaders who focus on making change in only one or several areas, while ignoring others, will be less successful in the long run.

Earlier in this text we talked about 360-degree thinking, which is not only a critical thinking competency for leaders but also an essential competency for viewing the eight organizational foundations as a system. Leaders need to ensure that they don't make decisions in a vacuum, that they understand the fundamental nature of the connections among the foundations and how together they affect an organization.

Consider, for example, an association that defines innovation and risk-taking among its core values and then fails to reward or praise staff or volunteer groups who take big risks in designing programs, products, or services. Leaders need to see the interconnections and practice more holistic execution of the key foundations of their organizations.

Most association leaders agree that the eight organizational foundations are important and acknowledge their individual presence. Most understand the need for interconnectedness among the foundations, but many have been struggling to achieve it. Christopher Seiz, executive director of the Long Beach Island (New Jersey) Foundation of the Arts and Sciences, recognizes the interconnectedness of the foundations and the need for a focus on all:

> These elements are interconnected in a way that is underemphasized in traditional thinking; that has the ability to significantly strengthen my organizational structures and create success for my organization. Without one [foundation], the organization will

rarely meet its goals. Every organization has its strengths and weaknesses in these areas. Finding the right balance given the times is what a leader must do. Reviewing the foundations enabled me to see that the people element was lacking within my organization and needed more focus.

An example of the interrelationships among the foundations can be seen in the experiences of one large association's strategic planning process. The association is comprised of more than 1,200 institutions, organizations, and individuals who develop programs in use at many colleges and universities in the United States and Canada. Essential to their successful strategic planning effort was an articulation of the association's core purpose. The association is a large and complex organization serving a large and complex professional interest area, and often its fundamental purpose was not universally understood by members, stakeholders, or the public, and not even fully understood internally by the organization's leadership. Articulation of purpose was among the most significant elements that the strategic planning process was able to achieve, and one of the most significant observations that came out of the process was that despite the complex role that this organization plays, it is in fact an association—a group of people and organizations coming together for a common purpose, possessing common values, and seeking to achieve common goals.

Another significant element in the process was the articulation of common and shared principles, since its many component groups share very different principles, values, and operating standards. The articulation of a common set of principles across the organization has significantly helped the association to sustain change, focus, and positive direction.

The element of people was also essential in this effort. The organization consists of a wide variety of stakeholders, both internal and external to the organization, and the understanding, respect, and recognition that was bestowed on people helped to sustain momentum and interest in the process over time.

One of the things that admittedly the organization may or may not have succeeded in was the process of priority selection. In hindsight, the organization's leaders admit that they may have taken on too much at once. But they were seeking to capitalize on the momentum of the effort and, over time, much has been achieved and sustained.

The impact on planet can be gauged in the context that the association's industry has a significant impact on the public in the United States and globally. Its policies are often models for other countries as they seek to create similar organizations serving similar needs.

Like this particular organization, many associations understand the nature of the eight organizational foundations and have made progress in institutionalizing them. But it seems as though many associations have focused on several and not all foundations, so we believe that there is room for broader focus in associations on each one and a greater understanding of the interdependencies among them.

After describing each of the organizational foundations, we provide a set of thought-prompting questions. Taken together, these can serve as an excellent diagnostic tool for association leaders to determine the degree to which their associations have the full set of foundations in place. Considered separately, they may be useful to leaders in determining gaps and possibilities for added focus.

Purpose

Purpose is the reason for an organization's existence. It is central to an organization and its work. It is the inspiration for an organization's priorities and gives meaning to its performance. It is timeless. It is not like a goal that is achieved; it is an ongoing statement of aspiration. While the organization's vision of the future (potential) and goals (priorities) will change over time and its methods for achieving them (processes) will certainly shift as well, its purpose is the singular aspect of the organization that will endure without fundamental change.

Purpose should be should be vital, visible, and valued:

- **Vital.** The best organizations are those that have a solid, unwavering understanding of who they are and why they exist and that they need to exist.

- **Visible.** The purpose of an organization should be so embedded in its culture and linked so directly to its priorities that anyone can clearly see and understand it.

- **Valued.** Purpose is more than a superficial statement about why the organization exists. Purpose is the basis from which the organization's priorities flow.

Organizations come together for a purpose, and this purpose is often stated in rudimentary form in the bylaws and described at greater length in the strategic plan. Many organizations create a mission statement, highlight it on their website, tweak it once in a while, and then lose sight of it when they set priorities. Most mission statements contain too much information about how the organization will achieve what it actually wants to achieve and not enough about why it exists.

Buried inside many mission statements, however, is the actual statement of purpose. In their seminal work of the 1990s, *Built to Last* (2002), Jim Collins and Jerry Porras assert that the core purpose of an organization should be expressed in a short, focused, timeless statement about why the organization exists.

Such a statement can be an enormous benefit for an organization, serving as a litmus test for deciding what to do and what not to do. In several organizations we have worked with, discussions about expansion into new business areas or evaluation of existing programs and services have centered on the idea that something may or may not be fundamentally related to the organization's purpose. That is not to say that associations can't engage in nondues revenue initiatives that help to support activities that support the purpose. But a purpose statement helps keep the focus on what is most central to the organization and those it serves. The importance of a clear statement of purpose is demonstrated by organizations that lose sight of what they were originally organized to do.

This is not to say that an association cannot refine its purpose as its industry or interest area changes. But organizations that forget their purpose run a risk of irrelevance become in danger of ceasing to exist, or, worse yet, maintaining an existence that does not create value for members and stakeholders.

Thoughts to Consider About Purpose

- Why does our organization exist?
- In a single sentence, what is our organization's purpose?
- What does purpose mean for our organization's culture?
- What value has our organization always created and what value could we never envision ceasing to create?
- Has our purpose adjusted with changes over time? Has it preserved a uniqueness of focus that gives our organization the courage to change?
- If someone were to look only at our organization's priorities (goals), what would they say our purpose is?
- If we were to ask our committees or other stakeholder groups about our organization's purpose, what would they say it is and why? Would they all say the same thing?

Principles

Principles are the shared values of an organization. It is critical for leaders, whether they are volunteer members or professional staff, to share the values of the organization they serve. If association leaders don't live and behave according to the values of the organization, they can be disruptive to the long-standing culture of the organization and can cause its priorities to fall out of alignment with the organization's purpose. Clearly defined principles, along with purpose, enable an organization to more easily decide what to do—and equally important, what not to do.

Principles are the bedrock of an organization. They are concise statements that guide the behavior of individuals within the organization. They are used consciously or unconsciously by the board, staff, committees, and task forces in every decision that the organization makes. In an effective association, all actions of the board, staff, and committees are governed by these values. If people consistently or even periodically violate these core values or principles, the organization may, in fact, be sowing the seeds for its own demise.

In the most effective organizations, principles are sacred. They are more than just words; they guide how the organization achieves its purpose, selects its priorities, and treats its people. Finally, principles must be shown. They are visible, embedded in the culture of the organization so that individuals not familiar with the organization can perceive them.

Unsuccessful organizations have disagreements over the organization's principles. Building consensus on values leads to clarity of purpose. It can strip away emotional confusion that blocks leaders from seeing what the true purpose of the organization is. Why are values important to leaders today? How can leaders benefit from a greater understanding of their own internal values systems? William C. Frederick, in *Values, Nature, and Culture in the American Organization* (1995), notes, "Leaders are not only the source but also the most important means of establishing organizational values. Leaders not only set direction for the organization, they also establish the means to achieve the goals. These represent the beliefs and behaviors that cannot be compromised for the sake of results. It is through this handle of values that leaders shape people's behavior and build organizational culture."

Frederick says that the role that leaders play in articulating values is essential to the success of any society, civilization, or organization. He believes that an understanding of one's values is also essential to the success of managers/leaders themselves.

Tim Hatcher of North Carolina State University, writing in Scott Quatro's book *Executive Ethics: Ethical Dilemmas and Challenges for the C Suite* (2008), notes,

> Today's CEO faces pressures unknown in earlier times.
> Globalization, market and economic turbulence, the challenges of
> new technologies, demographic and workforce shifts, the constant
> churn of change, and the myth of stability have transformed the

context and content of everything the executive does. In the organizations of today and the future, CEOs must articulate a clear vision that links his/her values with all stakeholder values and set the moral compass for the company. Executives are being challenged to connect their values with those of the organization, the industry, the community, and society.

When association leaders find themselves in situations where they must choose between conflicting outcomes that may require usurping their own values, what can they do? Without intimately understanding their own personal values and having a clear understanding of the extent that those values can and should be used to guide actions, it is easy for leaders to be forced into compromising situations and to make bad decisions.

John Townsend, PhD, in *Leadership Beyond Reason: How Great Leaders Succeed by Harnessing the Power of Their Values, Feelings, and Intuition* (2009), supports this assumption. He notes:

> Great leaders succeed by harnessing the power of both the external world and the internal world, and leaders are probably more trained, prepared, and experienced in the external world than in the inner one. .... There are several ways to describe what is beyond pure reason alone. Sometimes it is called the subjective, internal, or inner world. However, at the end of the day, it is simply one's immaterial life...passions, values, feelings, and intuitions, as well as thoughts. They cannot be seen or touched because they are not physical. But they are real, they exist, they are an essential part of the individual and they will be important to...success.

The effect of values on both individuals and organizations can be summarized as follows:

• Values have always been at the core of executive leadership and decision-making, and how leaders espouse those values has always been important.

• The values that leaders embrace have changed over time, driven in part by evolving management theories, organizational culture change, and changing societal norms.

- There is often a gap between espoused values of leaders and how they put those values into action. Sometimes leaders don't walk the talk, and the consequences can be significant.

- The kinds of decisions that association leaders are making today and will make in the future are increasingly complex. Leaders will no longer be able to rely solely on data-driven decision-making processes in times of turmoil, conflict, and change.

We believe it will become increasingly important for leaders to place greater dependence on their intuition and values to guide them in complex decision-making. While leadership capacities can be inherent and learned, we think that the most successful, inspiring leaders do not hold the belief that their reality is the true or only reality. The best leaders work to expand their knowledge of themselves while remaining flexible, continuously evaluating assumptions and adjusting as necessary their current perceptions versus perceived reality. They are open to information and knowledge but strive to balance it against their own internal principles, values, and belief systems.

Thoughts to Consider About Principles

- What are our organization's principles? How do we know these are our organization's principles?

- How do our organization's principles guide what we chose to do and chose not to do?

- How do our organization's principles affect how we treat our people?

- How are our organization's principles expressed to others within and outside of the organization?

- If someone were to observe our organization's actions and accomplishments, what would they say our principles are?

- If we were to ask our committees or other stakeholder groups about our organization's principles, what would they say they are and why? Would they all say the same thing?

- Do our principles and practices support change?

- What specific values are essential?
- What behaviors are associated with these values?

Potential

What do we mean by potential and why is it an organizational foundation? Potential is the achievement of the organization's vision, goals, and aspirational statements. As organizations dedicate themselves to reaching their full potential, they create the future in which they wish to exist by dedicating themselves to making their vision a reality.

Potential is reached by bridging the gap between where we are today and where we want to be tomorrow. Potential is the space of becoming; it's an awareness that there's an open space to fill, and defining what filling the space will ultimately achieve. Association leaders must ask themselves: What could we do or be? What do we have the potential of doing? What is possible but not yet achieved? What capacity for growth or development can we achieve as individuals and organizations?

According to Ideas for Action consultant Nancy Alexander, potential lives in the space between here and the vision, and realizing potential entails seeing the gap and harnessing the power, skills, and commitment to bridge that gap.

All associations have a vision, a view of what they are capable of accomplishing. These visions are formed through the association's experiences and the collective values, hopes, and dreams of leaders, members, stakeholders, and staffs. Organizations sometimes struggle with the balance between aspirations and reality. Leaders inspire their organizations to dream the impossible and motivate their members and staff to be something above and beyond what they are today.

Organizations can create a future that is beyond the current mindset of its members. Potential is a quest for continual improvement, continually reinventing how the organization achieves its purpose. So what does it mean for an organization to achieve its full potential? Can it ever truly be achieved? An interesting intellectual argument can be made about whether vision should be something that is achievable within a reasonable amount of time or whether vision is something that will never be possible.

In our work with organizations, we have found that the best visions are ones that are far enough out in the future to motivate, stimulate, energize, and enfranchise those who are a part of the organization. A vision statement that is already achieved does not serve the purpose of motivating anyone. Yet we see many organizations that continue to carry a vision statement that has been part of the organization's strategic plan for years, and when asked whether the vision has been achieved, they say, "Oh, yes!" We believe that espousing a vision that has already been achieved serves very little, if any, purpose. Vision statements must stretch the organization, its members, it stakeholders, and its industry or profession from what they have achieved today to what they seek to achieve in the future. If certain parts of an association's vision have already been accomplished, then perhaps it is time to re-examine the status and develop a new vision for the future.

A vision statement should reflect potential, paint a picture, or tell a story of how the world will be different and better as a result of what the organization achieves over time Vision needs to nurture an organization's potential for learning and growth; in fact, we believe this element of potential is particularly energizing. Organizations often miss an opportunity to engage and involve their stakeholders in achieving the organization's vision. An envisioned future with an audacious goal and vivid descriptions, as Jim Collins said in *Built to Last* (2002), can be a compelling talking point for an organization's leadership to engage volunteers and assist them in seeing how their contributions are creating a strengthened organization, profession, and industry.

Although much good work has been achieved in trying to evolve association governance systems, structures, processes, and cultures, it is still rare for an organization to be able to sustain a consistent vision of its potential over time, and even rarer that any two consecutive leaders, whether they be volunteers or staff, will see the path to that vision the same way. However, with an effective strategic plan and annual strategic plan review process, associations can ensure that successive leaders and boards become share a common direction and quest to achieve a long-term potential.

Good associations hold a strategic plan review and update session every year that allows the association's leaders to exercise 360-degree thinking by looking back on the past year to assess progress, look around to assess opportunities and threats in the current environment, and look ahead to set priorities for the coming year. If held at the point in the year where leadership changes and if the new, continuing, and departing board members all participate, the association creates the opportunity for a replenishment of the vision, a shared commitment to the direction, and a handing of the gauntlet to the next set of leaders to move down the path. In this way, association member leaders can adopt the sense that part of their role is to be stewards of the association's long-range vision, not to reinvent it to their own satisfaction. Consultant Nancy Alexander observes that when the right individuals are fully aligned with and energized by the organization's purpose, their potential and the organization's potential build on and reinforce each other.

Potential also implies an unleashing of a positive power, and this power is can be engaged most effectively and productively when the people within an organization are collectively committed to achieving potential and to focus on purpose and values as well. Obstructive patterns, power dynamics, and perceptions create friction and slow momentum; whereas, a clear, shared purpose acts as a touchstone and galvanizing force to achieve vision and potential.

Without potential, there is no future direction for an association. Without potential, an organization has no sense of when and how or whether it has achieved success. Organizations that focus on purpose and principles alone may not have a clear direction of where they are going. It is essential that organizations articulate a vision of what reaching their full potential will be like. It is also critical that organizations routinely reevaluate this vision, adjusting for relevance over time and assessing progress and movement toward achievement of that vision.

Thoughts to Consider About Potential

- Does our organization have an articulated vision statement?
- Does this vision statement clearly define what the organization and its environment would be like if full potential were reached?
- How is our vision for the future linked to our organization's purpose?
- How do our organization's principles influence our vision of the future?
- Is there widespread buy-in of this vision by volunteer and staff leadership?
- Would we know if we had reached our full potential? If we had, would we continue to keep our vision statements or declare success and move on to articulating a new vision?
- What outcomes is our organization able to achieve more effectively because of committing to our potential?

Process

Effective organizational processes are essential to the health of an organization and to its future. There are many good books on association, nonprofit, and corporate business processes, and in addressing this topic, we are merely framing the existence of processes as an essential foundation in successful organizations.

To be successful, associations must have repeatable processes that help individuals and groups understand and organize how work should be done and how objectives should be met. It is also critical that organizations have processes in place to define and measure success.

The concept of business processes for associations, while not new, is evolving. Associations have often created programs based on the good ideas of influential leaders, and over time the program and service portfolio becomes a cacophony of formerly good ideas. Associations that have put in place good business processes know how to evaluate the ongoing efficiency of programs and services and have underlying functional processes in place to manage the infrastructure that is required to deliver those products and services.

Many associations have also put in place processes to monitor and track success. These often include dashboard reports, strategy maps, priority mapping tools, and balanced scorecards. While these are all good measures, they also originated in the corporate environment, where work and decision-making processes are very different from the association world.

Dashboard reporting is a visual representation of how an organization is progressing toward achieving its priorities. It is a high-level snapshot of an organization's march toward sustained positive change. Dashboards can help create consensus, in writing, of the measurements used to define success. They can enable leaders, staff, and members to clearly know when success is achieved. Implementing dashboard reporting can be a natural evolution of a leadership team's conversation about what defines success. It also enables the organization to stay clearly focused on purpose and priorities. Linking a dashboard to the processes necessary to accomplish goals can help staff ensure that the organization's resources are aligned with its priorities. High-level information contained in dashboards can be used by the board of directors to evaluate progress toward accomplishing priorities, and department and functional measurements can be tied to staff performance evaluations, ensuring that everyone within the organization works toward the same goals.

In the association world, it is less likely than in the corporate sector that one individual will be able to make a decision relative to the execution of a task. Therefore, processes are essential to helping the combined workforce of staff and volunteers function effectively together.

Processes are important in associations because without them, it is hard to sustain progress. Without repeatable processes for delivering association services, such as conventions, webinars, magazines, newsletters, and the like, every time a process or program is executed, it may be done in a different way, with entirely different results. One of the challenges that associations already have is that volunteer leadership changes from year to year. In many organizations, volunteer workforces also change, and without the presence of repeatable sustained, institutionalized processes, there is little ability for the organization to capture institutional memory and consistency. The role of staff is essential in this retention, but the authority of staff to execute programs from organization to organization.

Among the most essential processes that an organization needs to sustain over time are strategic and operational planning. Without the continuity and commitment to long-term direction, an organization may lose sight of its purpose and potential and may drift. And without operational planning, its priorities may not be accomplished.

What tactics do successful organizations employ to institutionalize successful strategic and operational planning?

- Consideration of all key constituencies and staff and members working together;
- Inclusion, accepting that all ideas are important and that all contributions matter and are valued;
- Open communication;
- No predetermined outcomes;
- Ongoing commitment;
- Setting in writing bold and aggressive outcomes;
- Support of the plan by the association's executive staff and volunteer leaders;
- Constant communication and linking activities to the plan;
- Initial designation of individuals assigned to specific goals; and
- Accountability measures embedded in the plan.

The staff leadership of one large organization offers the following advice about processes to other associations and their leaders, gained through their strategic planning process:

- Ensure broad stakeholder input into the development of processes. Provide constant communication through the execution of tasks.

- After allowing stakeholders to have their voices heard during the collection of information stage, bring together the membership's senior leadership and ask those individuals to identify the deliverables they want.

- Pay attention to how thoughts are evolved during the input process to avoid losing the interest of stakeholders because they believe they have heard it all before.

- Assign clear accountabilities to staff groups. Ensure accountability and oversight, including the coordination of the work of smaller groups into the larger organization.

- Be aware that developing processes for a large organization takes more time and effort than may be anticipated.

Thoughts to Consider About Process

- What is the role of process in sustaining organizational change? What processes should be in place, and how does our association make them a sustained and positive part of our culture?

- Has our association institutionalized repeatable, effective processes?

- Do we have mechanisms for measuring progress toward our full potential?

- Have we institutionalized strategic and operational planning processes?

- Do those processes allow us to select priorities that move us toward our full potential?

- Are our processes aligned with our purpose and principles, and do we successfully engage and involve people in it?

Priorities

If there is one thing a membership organization has more of than members, it is ideas. As these ideas transform into strategies and then priorities, it is the responsibility of the board and chief staff officer to ensure that the organization's priorities are aligned with its purpose and principles.

One of the most difficult things for associations to do is maintain focus. Boards of directors should engage in critical conversations about what to do and, just as important, what not to do. There is generally no shortage of ideas within an association, but there are often limitations on resources of time, dollars, and people.

Successful organizations limit their focus to one or two strategic priorities at a time. Prioritization is not an exercise of creating a rank-ordered list of objectives and seeing how many can be checked off. Prioritization is selecting one or two new things that can make the greatest impact in a specific time and then devoting time, energy and resources to them. Effective prioritization happens as part of a strategic and operational planning process.

Organizations need to have a firm understanding of what they do well and what they don't. This understanding of core competencies and limiting factors assists organizations in making decisions about priorities. Even though organizations set priorities, they must remain flexible to respond to unforeseen opportunities, threats, and changes in the marketplace (environment) in which it and its members and stakeholders operate.

Good priorities have five characteristics:

• **Focused.** Must be tied to the organization's purpose;

• **Fit.** Must fit with the organization's core competencies, what it does well; fit with the organization's principles; and fit within the organization's limited resources;

• **Flexible.** Be able to adjust priorities based on new information or shifting needs of stakeholders;

• **Fact-based.** Choices based on research and data; and

- **Feel right.** Intuition blended with data when setting priorities. In leadership, intuition isn't simply a gut reaction; it is the art of blending knowledge with perception to make decisions. (This concept is explored in greater detail in our chapters on dynamic decision-making and intuition.)

Priority mapping is a tool organizations can use to align their limited resources to accomplish their priorities. For example, if an organization has identified redesigning its website as a priority and the marketing department is responsible for implementation, the organization may not look beyond the marketing department to realize the total amount of resources needed to accomplish this goal. In priority mapping, the organization would examine the impact not just to the marketing department but perhaps also to IT, membership, researchers, and other stakeholders. This mapping creates dialogue among staff, members, and volunteer leaders. It ensures staff and members are not working in silos. Many organizations work on priorities linearly; priority mapping is a holistic approach to understanding an organization's goals in light of its capacity. It informs organizational priorities and ensures organizational leaders are well aware of the impact on resources created by the decisions they make.

Thoughts to Consider About Priorities

- Do all our organization's priorities flow from our purpose? If not, which ones do not link to our purpose, and what should we do about that?

- What do we as an organization do well? How do these core competences affect what we chose to do or not to do?

- What do we as an organization not do well? How does this understanding affect what we chose to do or not to do?

- How do organizations that successfully sustain change decide what to focus on? How can our organization mimic their methods?

- What are the cultural implications of deciding not to do something? How do those decisions affect the direction and velocity with which our organization moves toward change?

- What are our resources and what are the existing limitations of those resources? How effectively are we using our resources? How does our understanding of our limited resources affect what we chose to do or not to do?

- Do we routinely evaluate our programs and services to ensure they align with our purpose and create value?

- How do we respond to unanticipated opportunities and threats?

People

In organizations, particularly service-based organizations, success largely depends on people and their level of engagement. Washington DC-based consultant Vinay Kumar notes, "The people portion tends to be the single biggest expense for most organizations, including associations. And without the right people on the team (who have the right technical and soft skills and fit the culture), hard results just don't happen. People are the capital and currency in associations. People generate ideas, energy, enfranchisement, and action."

People participate in associations for various reasons: to give back, to grow personally or professionally, to lead, to influence, and so forth. Association leaders who understand these underlying motivations will be successful. They will also help their associations create clear role distinctions for members, volunteers, and staff who are engaged in the work of the organization, respecting the unique skills, experiences, and expectations of each group.

One of the most important aspects of the people organizational foundation in successful associations is role clarity. Within associations, defining and building consensus around role distinction creates a sense of community. Within charitable organizations, this creates connections between stakeholders and the organization. When members focus on what members are good at doing, and staff focus on what staff are good at doing, great things happen!

In associations, misunderstandings about the roles people fill as members or staff can occur. This misalignment of views generally is a result of differing expectations relating to who is responsible for carrying out the tasks associated with the work of the organization.

An effective way for an association executive to communicate the ideal role of members and staff is to help people understand what each group is uniquely qualified to do. As a result, it is easy to create clear expectations and responsibilities for both groups.

Association members and staff bring different and equally desirable experiences, knowledge, and skills to an organization. Members bring a deep understanding of their profession, including issues, concerns, needs, and emerging environmental shifts; relationships within the industry; and a strong desire to engage in meaningful organizational work. Staff brings a set of technical and strategic skills relating to competencies of association management. These include meeting facilitation, understanding of governance, knowledge of association best practices, event planning, finance, and marketing, among many others.

The most successful organizations flourish in an environment where members and staff share, respect, and blend their knowledge, skills, expertise, and relationships to do the work of the association.

To maximize contributions of members and staff, an association's leaders must:

- Understand the unique skills, expertise, and relationships of members and staff;

- Understand how to leverage these factors;

- Clearly define in writing the roles and expectations for all new projects and in all committee work;

- Genuinely respect and appreciate the different things each group brings to the organization;

- Ensure open dialogue based on trust and in alignment with the organization's purpose and principles; and

- Ensure the skills of members and staff are aligned with the tasks they are asked to perform.

Many associations craft written committee charges. These are typically short, written lists of bullet points that outline a committee's work for the year. The charges state the committee's goals but not how it will accomplish its objectives. The charges tie directly back to the association's purpose, potential, and priorities. Successful organizations have committee charges outlining the role of staff in helping member committees accomplish work on programs or projects. This reinforces role distinction and ensures everyone knows who is responsible for what before starting to work together.

Thoughts to Consider About People

- What are our understandings about the roles that people play in our organization's board, committees, and staff? How do we develop a shared understanding of these roles?

- How do the organization's purpose, practices, and principles affect how people are regarded, how leaders lead, and how members, staff, and customers are treated?

- What are the unique skills, knowledge, and relationships that members bring to the organization?

- What factors allow people to become fully engaged in change?

- Do we clearly communicate to members and staff before the start of a project who is responsible for what and why?

- What should the board do and what should it delegate?

- Is the board of directors empowered to govern the organization?

- Is the chief staff officer empowered to manage the organization?

- Are committees and other stakeholder groups empowered to do the work that they have been delegated, within parameters set by the board?

- How do we ensure that the skills of our members are aligned with the roles in which we ask them to serve?

Praise

The role of praise in an organization is essential. Associations and other nonprofit organizations operate on volunteer commitment and staff passion. Without praise, without validation, without reward and recognition, the energy in volunteerism and staff dedication will die. There are two important forms of praise in organizations: internal and external. Internal praise deals with recognizing members, staff, and stakeholders for their contributions to the organization.

When thanking individuals for their efforts, it is important to be specific, rather than general. When thanking people for specific behavior, it is essential to help them understand what they did well, encouraging more of that behavior in the future. Rather than giving a general compliment such as, "Thank you for your great work on the membership campaign," it is important to clearly identify what the individual specifically did well and its effect on the organization.

Educational psychologist Stephen Brock, PhD, of Kennesaw State University, developed a model showing how to do just that. In the Kennesaw State (Georgia) Executive MBA curriculum, Brock identifies this model as BET (Behavior, Effect, Thank You). For example, "Erin, when you created talking points for volunteers to use when making phone calls to prospective members, you enabled them to gain confidence in what they were saying and also ensured there was a consistent approach to our membership recruitment campaign. Thank you."

In addition to thanking individuals, it is also important to recognize the contributions of groups such as committees. The organization should also communicate successes to all members and other stakeholders, because when members see public recognition of the association's successes, it helps to create a culture of engagement and an environment where members feel genuinely appreciated for their contributions to the organization.

It is also important for organizations to seek external validation through awards, media coverage, and government procla-mations. Doing so further develops a culture of success and also reinforces that the organization is creating and delivering value to its stakeholders. It demonstrates that an organization has strong processes of organizational governance and management.

One of the challenges in successful organizations is that the greater the level of success, the higher the bar is raised for the future. In these situations, it is even more critical for leaders to express praise routinely and with genuine appreciation.

Thoughts to Consider About Praise

- What role do praise, recognition, and valuing contributions play in our association?

- What are the implications of celebrating success, even if we are still part way along the journey?

- How does our organization express appreciation for member contributions and accomplishments?

- How does our organization express appreciation for staff contributions and accomplishments? Do our methods of rewarding staff reflect what they value as recognition of their contributions?

- How does our organization communicate and celebrate organizational accomplishments?

- What opportunities are there for our organization to achieve external validation through awards, media coverage, government proclamations, and such?

- When we thank individuals for their contributions, do we recognize specific behaviors?

Planet

Planet is an understanding that the fulfillment of an organization's purpose and potential can create a ripple effect in the world around it. Leaders who understand this can see that what they do can have results beyond the organization itself.

Carrie Mattingly, utilities director for the city of San Luis Obispo California, notes: "We're the organizational cheerleaders for embracing what we call the triple bottom line (social, economic, and environmental—or people, planet, and prosperity). We are invigorated by our purpose in that it positively impacts and attracts a community of people who are out to change the world in which they live. By managing the community's water supply, we keep them healthy so they can do this!"

A trade association realized that one of its long-standing training programs could be configured and used for workforce training for people who are unemployed. As a result, it secured federal funding for unemployed workers to participate in the program as a way to gain new job skills. It brought more newly trained people into the industry and also enabled the organization to make a positive impact on its community.

The implications of the decisions that an association leaders makes often extend beyond the organization to the world around the organization, whether it be the community, the industry, the country, or the planet. Leaders far too often miss the big picture, and failing to see the big picture can result in achieving the wrong picture. As an organization reaches its full potential, it can create positive change in the world at large.

Shelly Alcorn, CAE, in a white paper titled "Association Executives: Provocative Proposals for Change" (2012), identified some of the attitudes of association leaders regarding their impact on the world at large:

> Interviewees strongly felt they make a demonstrable impact on society, particularly in regards to local, state and national economics, public health and education. A number of interviewees expressed their belief that they have a significant responsibility to help the public understand what their members do and why their members make life better for society. Other interviewees felt a strong sense of responsibility to impact the public directly and expressed a desire to look beyond their membership borders and work for the good of all, not necessarily just their members. Establishing certification programs, setting standards and encouraging or enforcing ethical behavior were mentioned most often as tangible outcomes of these efforts.

Many associations have an awareness of and commitment to creating a positive impact on the world around them, even at a local level. For example, ASAE routinely engages in local community service projects in the communities where major meetings are held. Planet is about having an awareness of the world outside the association and its membership, and we believe this fundamental foundation will become even more important in the future. As the business and regulatory environment of associations in the United States comes under greater pressure, there will be an even greater need for associations to demonstrate a commitment to affecting the greater good in the world around them.

Thoughts to Consider About Planet

- How would the world be different if our organization didn't exist?

- How do we create value for our members and stakeholders?

- How does what we do effect the community outside our organization?

- What are the ripple effects of the programs and services we provide?

- What opportunities that align with our purpose and principles do we have to create positive change not just within our organization but also within the world?

- How does our organization connect with the world around it?

PART III

One Unifying Strategy— Co-Creation

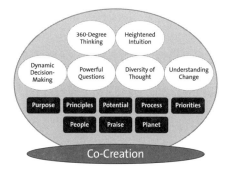

CHAPTER 8

Co-Creating the Future: How Leaders Lead Together

ONCE THE EIGHT ESSENTIAL foundations are in place in an organization and leaders have developed deeper capacity in each of the six emerging leadership competency areas, how do they think, lead, and achieve? How do they take advantage of a broader set of ideas and a steadier flow of energy into their organizations? They engage in one unifying strategy—co-creation of the future of their organizations.

Co-creation in the corporate sector refers to a lasting partnership between a company and its customers, a partnership that creates value for both. But what does co-creation mean for the association community? How do association leaders make co-creation a reality? What does it mean to say that co-creation is partnership between people at all levels of the organization? Why is co-creation necessary to create lasting change?

Association leaders are constantly working to create engagement, involvement, and collaboration among volunteers and staff. However, given our interruption-driven culture, where we are exposed to so many stimuli at the same time and are susceptible to interrupting whatever it was we were doing, enfranchisement tends to be short-lived and collaboration is no longer sufficient. In any truly successful organization, co-creation is much more valuable than lesser forms of engagement. Through co-creation, association leaders and their stakeholders at all levels can develop and sustain a deeper partnership.

Three Levels of Co-Creation

Washington, DC-based Consultant Vinay Kumar identifies three levels of engagement that exist in associations:

- **Level 1: What's in it for me?** This is the basic foundational level of engagement, where each individual (member, staff, or volunteer) is first thinking about what's in it for him or her. For staff, this motivation includes income, benefits, a position with clear responsibilities, the opportunity to use one's talents and abilities, work that provides growth and development, a reasonable commute, and a nice work environment. Members and volunteers may be seeking education, networking, and opportunities to lead and influence—elements that help them do better in their individual careers and businesses.

- **Level 2: What's in it for you?** Once our basic needs are met and we are secure at the first level, we begin to think more in terms of the factors external to ourselves. Thus, staff may begin to think more about what the members and volunteers want and need, and members and volunteers begin to think about the staff's wants and needs. This is engagement, collaboration, and involvement, but work at this level tends to be issue-specific and ephemeral, not sustained and permanent.

- **Level 3: What's in it for us?** This is the highest level of engagement. When we begin to work at this stage, we start to see the interconnectedness of ourselves and our colleagues, and we realize that when we serve others, we also serve ourselves.

In our experience, at the third level of engagement, following elements are present:

• Shared purpose;
• Shared values;
• Mutual understanding, respect, appreciation, and trust;
• Clear roles and responsibilities; and
• Open dialogue based on mutual trust and respect.

At this level, we understand more about what each person brings to the mix and what value each adds. We leverage and appreciate each other, and we care about each other's well-being. We finally see that we are all in the same boat, rowing together toward the same destination, and we share in reasons for doing what we're doing. At this stage, our efforts are multiplied and everyone wins together.

For an association to function at the third stage requires clear role distinctions for members, volunteers, and staff engaged in the work of the organization and respect for the unique skills, experiences, and expectations of each group. It is our experience that within associations, defining and building such consensus around role distinction also creates a sense of community.

A Continuum of Connection and Commitment

Co-creation takes on a number of forms in the association environment. It happens among staff and member leaders. It happens between leadership and members. It happens in committees and in staff work groups. And it happens individually, in the minds and hearts of all those who engage in work for your organization.

FIGURE 7. *The Path to Co-Creation as a Continuum of Connection and Commitment*

Co-creation is the deepest form of commitment among members and staff within an association. It is an organizational environment in which input from staff and member leaders is equally important, resulting in a deeper, stronger leadership partnership. Shared ownership of an outcome is emphasized over individual ownership of ideas.

It can be assumed that by virtue of joining, a member begins to engage in an association. The introductory level of connection and commitment between a member and an association takes on a variety of forms, including attending an educational program, conference, or networking event; purchasing an association product or service; or reading the association's communications, either print or electronic. Many associations invest considerable funds to engage members in these ways.

Engagement, however, is not lasting. The simple transactional nature of these relationships between an association and its members mirrors what is seen in the marketplace between companies and customers. Members may engage with your association today and with another organization tomorrow. They may choose what events, activities, and benefits are of value to them at any given moment. Engagement between members and associations, while desirable, does not yield long-term benefits and does not necessarily lead to a relationship that includes co-creation. This first-level relationship and some of the themes in the following paragraphs are examined in some detail in ASAE's book *The Decision to Join* (2007) and the more recent ASAE Foundation Research Series publication *10 Lessons for Cultivating Member Commitment: Critical Strategies for Fostering Value, Involvement, and Belonging* (2012).

The next step on the continuum is involvement. Associations seek, value, and often cultivate members who are committed to active involvement in the organization. This involvement may include not only regular attendance at conferences, accessing programs and services, and participation in awards or networking programs but also volunteering to help make those programs successful. These activities may encourage a deeper level of partnership between members and the staff of the association, but they are still somewhat transactional in nature.

The third step of the continuum is collaboration. In an effective partnership, staff and volunteers may work together, or collaborate, on a variety of program areas, tasks, and activities. Collaboration is a deeper level of commitment because members are investing their time, ideas, and dollars in the organization. However, even at this level, members may collaborate within the association but may not form a deep connection with its purpose, principles, potential, and priorities.

The continuum's next step is investment. Investment goes beyond engagement, involvement, and collaboration because there is a deeper enfranchisement, an incentive for continuing the dialogue and the relationship. The member is concerned with the outcome and is aligned with the organization's purpose, principles, priorities, and potential. At this step in the continuum, members begin to build an emotional connection to the association's activities, outcomes, and success. Investment requires a deeper level of connection; it calls for individuals and organizations to listen in a deeper way.

The final step in the continuum is co-creation. Co-creation involves all of the previous partnerships and behaviors, plus a shared commitment to combine and use the collective resources and capabilities of the partnership, creating value for the association and its stakeholders. Co-creation requires imagination, ingenuity, and new ways of thinking, often yielding new forms of interaction, service, and learning. It occurs when participants are equally valued in terms of what they bring, who they are, and to what they are committed and enables member and staff leaders to co-create the future together. These leaders operate in an environment where the foundations of the organization are in place and they are exercising the six emerging leadership competencies, then imagine the possibilities for the future in their work together.

The Role of Leadership in Co-Creation

Co-creation is not just the influence of a single leader with a good idea. It's not staff simply going along with whatever member leaders are seeking to achieve. Co-creation is a state of collaboration that is much deeper than what has been achieved in most associations.

What is the role of an association's chief staff officer in co-creation? There are three common models of association leadership, and the model used by an organization greatly affects how and if co-creation is achieved. These models include the board chair as chief executive or decision-maker, the executive/staff director as the chief executive, and the balanced model partnership where the role is shared. Below is a short review of each model.

Board chair as chief executive. In this model, the board chair is the face of the membership and the external face of the organization. In some industries and professions, this is preferable because the chief executive position garners greater credibility in areas like advocacy when someone from the industry or profession is in the more visible role. In this model, the chief staff executive's role is to manage the internal organization and to be a witness to and a participant in the creation of strategy, direction, and prioritization but not necessarily to be a full partner in their development.

Chief staff executive as chief executive. When the chief staff executive acts as CEO, he or she plays both an internal and external role. Volunteer leadership entrusts this individual not only to oversee internal operations but also to be the external face of the organization. Making this model work requires shared commitment to purpose, principles, priorities, and potential on the part of the chief staff executive and the board. Co-creation is possible with this model. However, we are aware of many organizations where the chief staff executive and staff drive the agenda to some extent and consult the volunteer leaders to keep them informed. This situation may produce efficient operations, but it is not co-creation.

Balanced partnership. The third model requires an excellent working relationship between the chief staff and chief elected officers. Because many board terms change regularly, this relationship requires a constant renegotiation, re-evaluation, reforming, and reconnection of priorities and work processes between the two leadership partners. It requires excellent communication, a commitment to a shared agenda and priorities, a good understanding of each other's working and thinking styles, and a commitment to hold the association's priorities higher than personal priorities. Many associations strive to achieve this third model, but the ingrained systems, structures, and culture in many organizations results in the chief elected officer's playing a more significant role in leadership and priority setting.

The choice among these models may be affected by the maturity of the mission of the organization. If your organization has an evolved, ingrained mission that has strengthened over time, you can live with the rapid turnover of volunteer leadership, and the second or third models become the best choices. If the organization lacks long-term commitment to its mission, then none of the three will be sufficient over time and the association will become like a boat tossed in the wind, constantly changing individual leaders and priorities. That's why the foundations of purpose, principles, potential, and priorities are so important.

Sometimes co-creation is not possible, especially when executives and associations have ceased to be a good match or when there's been a breakdown of trust. In the most successful organizations, there is an enormously high trust level between board and staff, an understanding of and commitment to shared principles. It is in this environment where true co-creation is possible. It is far beyond the nomenclature of staff driven, or member driven, or even knowledge driven. It's just about being driven. Another way to express this concept is to recognize that staff and members share a common destiny in serving their organization—that they are truly in it together.

Some have said that the association executive's job is to lead without getting caught. This concept is problematic to others, as it seems inauthentic. It also doesn't fit with the concept of co-creation. Co-creation feels more authentic to many leaders because it is a situation where neither staff nor member is trying to influence from the side but both openly and collectively dialogue and create the future together.

In organizations where leaders practice the emerging competencies and have all of the organizational foundations in place and top of mind, co-creation is a constant. It is not swayed, deterred, or derailed by the next set of volunteer leaders with different priorities, by new staff who do not possess organizational memory, or by new priorities that may take the association in a different direction. It is constant. It is simply an accepted, valued, and essential part of the association's culture.

Co-Creation Breaks Down Organizational Silos

Another benefit of co-creation is that in large organizations, co-creation erases the silos that occur among departments, divisions, subsidiaries, affiliated foundations, chapters, and other organizational components. It also creates synergy between an association's committees, task forces, and other workgroups.

Silos are often the result of staff and volunteer leaders who think and act primarily from the viewpoint of what is best for the organizational component they represent. Leaders who inspire co-creation enable everyone to see beyond their individual interests and to focus on the organization's strategic direction and how their contributions assist in co-creating the envisioned future of the association.

As staff and member leaders in an association become more fully invested in the association, they build a shared vision of the organization's future and see how their priorities and objectives tie to the strategy of the organization as a whole. Then silos begin to break down, and co-creation starts to occur. This results in a reduction of internal resource battles among organizational components. The same powerful results are achieved among member/volunteer leaders.

Without a shared commitment to the organization's full potential and vision, without the use of 360-degree thinking, dynamic decision-making, the power of a question, and the other emerging leadership competencies, co-creation cannot occur in large organizations, and separate departments will forever be battling for resources, attention, and recognition. This may even happen in smaller staff organizations if staff feels more connected to a specific agenda than to the overall purpose, principles, priorities, and potential of the full organization.

Co-creation allows great things to happen. Associations accomplish their goals and achieve their envisioned future when staff and member leaders work together in equal partnership. Co-creation occurs when the organization is able to create a culture where members and staff feel equally invested in both the outcome and the in the creation of that outcome.

Co-creation is a competency, a tool, and a mindset. Co-creation at the board level equates with complete engagement in strategy, planning, and strategic dialogue. Many organizations have been working toward this co-creative culture for years. But to create and sustain positive change, co-creation needs to become a permanent element of the culture, and leaders need to think in new ways.

Co-Creation in Decision-Making

Aside from the defining co-creation in terms of enfranchisement and working together, co-creation can be defined by the role it plays in individual and group decision-making. It can be said that there are three kinds of decisions: command, where one person has the authority and accountability to make the decision; consultative, where the decision is still to be made by one person, but that person seeks input and engages others in the process; and consensus, where decisions must be made by a full group and not an individual.

Real issues can arise when these distinctions are not clear. Groups expecting to co-create may find that a decision has already been made and may feel totally disenfranchised. Consider the board chair who felt that it was in her purview to make a unilateral decision without consulting the board or the board that was asked to ratify a decision that had already been made by the executive committee. Co-creation cannot exist when there is insufficient clarity about who is making decisions.

Case Study: Co-Creating the Future

In times of crisis, smart leaders are able to effect policy, practice, and culture change in ways that, when examined in retrospect, can become game changers—profound, institutionalized, and lasting. The following case study of Building Owners and Managers Association of Georgia illustrates achieving success through co-creation, despite challenges to the association's marketplace and economic future.

Several years ago, during the height of the recent economic downturn that crippled the United States and world economies, there was one quote that seemingly fell off the lips of economic experts and politicos everywhere: "Never let a crisis to go to waste. It's an opportunity to do things you could not do before." By now, we have all become acquainted with "the new normal," how things went downhill during the recession and how new realities have forced us to settle for less going forward.

But even through difficult times, some associations have been able to change the way they do business while improving the value they deliver to members. One vital key to achieving this kind of success is effective staff and member leadership, encompassing collective vision, energy, and focus.

Despite weathering the worst of times for the commercial real estate industry, the staff and member leaders of BOMA Georgia focused on enhancing the success of commercial real estate professionals and worked in partnership to achieve significant results. Over four years, the association increased membership each year, growing 21 percent. It also grew event attendance 33 percent and expanded revenue 21 percent. In an industry where percentages count, BOMA Georgia increased education enrollment by 213 percent. That's no typo; you are reading it correctly—213 percent. As other associations struggled to keep things at the status quo, what contributed to this association's success?

One of the key factors was the transition to an enabling, effective, and energizing governance culture of co-creation. This transformation enabled BOMA Georgia to achieve tremendous growth, unprecedented success, and accomplishment of its key strategic initiatives.

The organization also implemented several new strategic initiatives, including developing a human resources management certificate program, training for medical office building managers, young professionals' events, and a new grassroots advocacy system.

They also partnered with their international affiliate to create and launch the "Foundations of Real Estate" course, a comprehensive educational program designed for property professionals.

During the execution of these impressive results, while this association was going through a critical organizational change, so was its young executive director. Promoted from within, and stepping into the role during difficult times for the association, his success and that of his organization are undoubtedly interconnected, and the story is a compelling one.

"Our executive director has brought about trust, loyalty, and undying support among not only our leadership and staff but our entire membership as a whole," said one BOMA Georgia member. "BOMA would not be where it is today without the leadership and guidance of our CEO. He has made our association strong financially and has earned the respect of the entire membership. The best decision we ever made was to put him in charge, and there is no end to his talent."

Several years earlier, this organization was at a crossroads. It had survived management transitions and financial turbulence. There were often issues of trust between staff and member leaders. Members questioned the value of the organization, and the association was not moving forward strategically. There was no shortage of effort, but each effort acted alone instead of in concert toward a key objective. There was no dominant, long-term goal other than to simply exist.

Fortunately, there was a strong group of committed volunteers. Leaders were willing to grow and change, even if that change were to cause some short-term pain. And there was an understanding among the leaders that they needed to refocus to become a greater organization.

Over the years of change, a new, enabling culture took hold, and as the current association president, says members can't help but notice the positive transition, be excited about it, and want to be a part of it.

"The changes are significant. There are only a few of us who remember what it was like before we operated under strategic governance. Before, you'd attend a board meeting and everything was already decided on and approved. Board members didn't feel as though they had a whole lot of input."

Leaders who were involved in leadership during the transition, also acknowledge the positive outcomes of the change orchestrated by the CEO. The board has transitioned to a format of strategic governance and co-creation, from an operational model. Before, it considered mostly operational issues and annual programs without thinking about where to take the organization in the near future and in years to come.

Since beginning this transformational journey, the association has implemented a strategic long-range plan that identified what the organization had not been doing in the past and what it must be doing in the future to be successful. Their strategic thinking model of governance now considers short-term goals, while working towards achieving big goals encompassing 10- to 30-year visions. The association's ability to focus on deliberate and strategic growth has allowed the organization to enjoy a culture of sustained success.

"At the end of each year, we have a laundry list of success stories because we begin each year with clearly defined objectives and we have the tools and support from our board to get those things done," says the organization's director of communications and marketing. "After we have defined these objectives, we rely heavily on our members and committees to take these goals and get them done through another tier of strategic planning. And in my experience, I've found that success breeds more success. Once we finish one priority, we reset our focus and move on to the next thing. It's exciting to navigate through these processes because you can look at our organization historically and see exactly what we have accomplished each year."

What role did staff leadership play in this organization's success? The story becomes even more complex when the tenure of the association executive is factored in.

The executive director was internally promoted, previously serving as communications director for less than two years. Making the move into the top staff leadership role, he had to balance two equally daunting tasks—transforming the organization's culture while simultaneously making his own career transformation. As he was shaping his own transition strategies, he also had to assemble a new staff team, which has also been key to the organization's success. The staff now consists of six full-time employees, including the executive director.

"I wanted to create a culture of inclusion and co-creation, a culture where we as staff would share in and be committed to the organization's success," says the executive director. "I also focused on role clarity between members and staff and on creating an environment where the board focuses on strategy, priorities, and vision rather than on getting into the details of staff and committee work. I believe that success comes most effectively when members and staff are each given the autonomy to do what they do best."

"Our staff is second to none," says the communications director. "Each staff member knows what they are responsible for and to what capacity they are lending their expertise toward the overall well-being of the organization. This allows each staff member to contribute in equal but separate ways. It allows staff members to stay focused; and it helps keep our office free from petty office politics. We each bring different ideas and considerations to the table, all while understanding that the reason we exist is to increase the professionalism and value of our members."

Another change strategy was to encourage the board to focus on only one or two strategic priorities at a time. Every year, with the facilitation and counsel of outside consultants, the board takes two days to meet as a group and plan for the upcoming year.

"The focus of this retreat is to determine where we are as an organization, where we have been, and where we have yet to go— and grow," said a staff leader. "And then, specifically, we select two strategic goals for the following year. Focusing only on these two large-scale goals in a given year assures that we are able to meet the everyday demands and needs of our members while maintaining forward progression."

Many associations struggle with success because they try to do too many things too quickly and without focus. At BOMA Georgia, an organized and focused governance structure allows the board of directors to be creative and develop ideas in a way that ensures the association's growth without taking on too much too fast.

Another key strategy was positioning strategic governance as a tool to build trust between the board and staff. "It was a long process," the executive director says. "But one way we were able to make progress was by introducing the idea that we co-create together. We as a staff share a common destiny with the organization. If the organization is successful, we're successful in sharing that success with members, recognizing and valuing the strengths that members and staff bring to the organization, and celebrating accomplishments such as achieving goals and milestones."

Here are lessons from BOMA Georgia's experience:

• **Focus on the foundation of potential.** Create a shared vision of the future. The board of directors and senior staff should collaborate to produce a written, focused, strategic plan. If they create the plan together, the vision they share about what success will look like is something they all will buy into.

• **Ensure the foundation of the governance process is based on proven association management theory.** Consult *The Will to Govern Well* (2002; second edition 2011) and bring in external experts to facilitate the process of change and to advise and consult about best practices in other associations. Begin to focus on strategy and making knowledge-based decisions as a routine part of doing business.

• **Ensure the foundation of potential is well understood.** Define success. Create a shared understanding of what success will look like in advance of each year, and put expectations in writing. Membership numbers, event attendance, education enrollment, and other association benchmarks may go up or down in a given year. However, if an association implements effective strategies, over time these benchmarks will all trend upward.

• **Ensure that priorities are clear.** No association can do everything at once. Choose a maximum of two strategic priorities each year, and don't try to tackle the entire strategic plan in one year.

- **Manage ideas but maintain focus.** One of the most important—and difficult—things for an association to do is maintain focus. If there is one thing an association has more of than members, it is ideas. Members often share many great, and some not-so-great, ideas with the association's leadership. Some members become discouraged if their ideas are not implemented and they don't understand why. Discussing the need for organizational focus is a powerful tool to help members understand the strategic direction of the association.

- **Enable co-creation through a clear understanding of roles**. Create a shared understanding of the roles of the board, committees, and staff and discuss roles before implementing projects. The most successful organizations flourish in an environment where both members and staff share, respect, and blend their knowledge, skills, expertise and relationships to do the work of the association.

- **Focus on people and employ the competency of diversity** of thought by empowering others. The board should empower committees and staff to implement the strategic priorities and the ongoing work of the organization.

- **Employ 360-degree thinking** by consistently sharing information from a variety of perspectives. The board and executive director should be transparent in making decisions, and those decisions should be based on shared principles and a mutual view of the future. This is a key to building trust within the organization.

- **Practice the organizational foundation element of praise.** Celebrate success. Routinely celebrate achieving goals and milestones with members and staff. This helps build a culture of inclusion and fun.

Thoughts to Consider About Co-Creation

- What does it mean to say that co-creation is a partnership between people all across an organization?

- How do we create an atmosphere that encourages the open exchange of ideas?

- How do we express the value of ideas, regardless of who comes up with them?

- How do we foster a shared ownership of organizational goals and outcomes?

- Why is co-creation necessary to create lasting change?

- How do we ensure partnerships where there is truly a shared investment and commitment to success?

- How can we make co-creation a reality? How do we get to the third level of thinking about "us" in balanced partnership together?

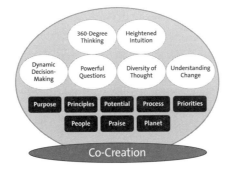

CHAPTER 9

What Gets in the Way: Barriers to Success

L
EADERSHIP IS POWERFUL. BUT it's also logical. That is to say, it should be logical. The competencies and foundations we have described in this book are logical, rational, and doable. What are the barriers that prevent leaders from looking at the big picture, from integrating all they know, making good group decisions, and co-creating the future? What individual and organizational behaviors get in the way of achieving positive change?

Chapter 6 explored individual beliefs, values, assumptions, and fears as key drivers or detractors of change. But there are reasons that change and positive momentum brought in by individual leaders don't always result in organizational success.

Although individuals may gain new skills and competencies, if the organization's systems, structures, processes, and cultures don't support the practice of these new skills, knowledge is lost and leaders cannot effectively grow. As you seek to implement the foundations and competencies in this book, both individually and organizationally, we caution you to be aware of the following organizational dynamics that may hinder your efforts:

Personality-Based Leadership

In organizations that are still subject to personality-based leadership, agendas, decisions, and actions can be driven by self-interest. There is the potential for limited group understanding and limited shared awareness. Diversity of thought, 360-degree thinking, powerful questions and other competencies cannot be practiced openly if the leadership culture as a whole does not support this kind of thinking. Personality-based leadership can hinder an association's ability to see the world from the broader perspectives needed for future success.

Pet Projects

When priorities are set because of an individual leader's agenda, rather than because of a cohesive holistic view of association priorities and strategies, the association's resources may be in danger of being spent on ideas that may or may not bring return to the association's members or the larger community. And asking powerful questions that may yield answers contrary to an individual leader's personal interests may be problematic. Pet projects may also exist in situations when too much intuition and not enough data have gone into a decision to invest the association's resources on a particular program or service.

Politics, Polarization, and Posturing

When an association's culture is driven by political dynamics—when decisions are driven by individual advocacy for the best idea rather than collective analysis and insight, by minimal use of data and information, and by pitting various constituencies against each other—an association cannot see the broader picture and practice leadership competencies effectively. When associations become divided, with groups taking strong positions and not sufficiently listening to others, leadership competencies may not be enough to achieve the desired results. When individuals take particular positions to benefit themselves rather than the organization as a whole, they are engaging in posturing.

Protecting the Past

Leaders in many organizations seek to protect the past, what they are invested in. Yet that may no longer work or may not be likely to work in the future. The future will bring exponential change, so protecting the past will not yield any positives. Leaders in successful organizations must give up personal ownership of things that may not be relevant in the future.

Many leaders and organizations have made great strides in eliminating some of these barriers from their organizational cultures. But one of the strange dynamics of associations is that as volunteer and staff leadership change, so may the maturity level and acceptance of culture. Regardless of how far forward an association may have been able to evolve, it is always possible that years later, when new leadership emerges on either the staff or the volunteer side, forward direction may be reversed.

As stated in Ken Blanchard's *Management of Organizational Behavior* (2007), there are four distinct stages in team development: forming, storming, norming, and performing. No matter how successful a group has been in achieving a level of high performance, one new person changes the dynamic and there is the potential for everything to go back to zero. And often when new individuals come into positions of power, even after an organization has had long and sustained positive change, some of the better behaviors that have been established are the very ones that are lost.

So we encourage association leaders to be aware of the potential for these setbacks and to continually educate, empower, and connect both staff and volunteer leadership with a consistent set of values, actions, behaviors, and competencies that will help your association sustain positive change and not take steps backward.

.

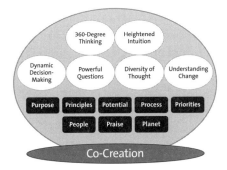

CHAPTER 10

Ideas for Action: How to Think, Lead, and Achieve in Your Organization

THIS BOOK HAS OUTLINED six emerging competencies that association leaders must have to create and sustain positive change, eight essential organizational foundations that must be in place for associations to be successful, and one unifying strategy for member and staff leaders to co-create the future together.

So how best to get started? In addition to the thought-prompting questions at the end of each chapter, we offer these guidelines for action:

Adopt a More Holistic/Multidimensional Leadership View

Leaders must adopt a holistic, multidimensional organizational view of leadership. The organizational foundations and competencies contained in this book might be considered new and different but are, in fact, quite natural. To harness the natural instincts of a leader, begin by challenging all assumptions.

Leaders must also think beyond commonly held expectations, priorities, and opportunities to find their organization's true potential. One of the elements that Keegan and Lahey talk about in *Immunity to Change* (2007) is the idea of adaptive challenge. Leaders must adapt to what is going on, not to their inherent and learned knowledge about what they expect to work or don't expect to work.

The identification of adaptive leadership and adaptive challenges includes the idea that leaders must confront their underlying fears and challenge their underlying assumptions about situations. We believe that doing so will help you to think in new and more complex ways.

Get Acquainted With Your Values and Intuition
Leaders must develop greater understanding of their own values and grasp how those values affect their behavior, decisions, and actions. Beyond this, leaders must also learn to read their intuition. While many leaders have been trained to simply use a data-driven approach in problem solving, leaders must learn to leverage their values and intuition when considering actions. Leaders must do this despite initial skepticism from those who are not familiar with the concept of dynamic decision-making.

Values clarification and understanding of individual and organizational culture can be accomplished with the help of executive assessments and tools and through work with an executive coach. Coaches can help leaders understand the deeper dynamics of how their personalities, values, and internal systems affect their performance as leaders.

When workplaces are filled with a mix of individuals from various cultures, generations, life experiences, and professional experiences, those workplaces become less homogenous and more filled with varying thoughts, perspectives, and feelings. So we believe that any leader in any organization would be well served by understanding more about the concepts of emotional intelligence. Goleman's work can serve as an excellent resource for this, and there are many talented executive coaches and leadership consultants who can work with your organization using assessments and tools that measure leaders' emotional intelligence. The concept of emotional intelligence is very different from other personality assessments and intelligence assessments. Your IQ score is a hardwired thing; experts say that it is not particularly changeable over time. But emotional intelligence skills can be improved. Experts say that working with leaders to help them understand, embrace, and use positive and productive emotions in the workplace can help create more informed and successful organizations.

Develop Dynamic Decision-Making Skills

Leaders must always trust their own intuition and values and must use them in both individual and group decision-making settings. Dynamic decision-making will help you quickly determining whether the incorporation of intuition is appropriate. It is not that leaders need to simply use intuition more often; it is that they need to understand when it is appropriate to use it along with data.

Leaders must not lose sight of the possibilities for shared intuition. Leaders can help groups to achieve group intuition by staying in tune with the values, intuition, and perceptions of their members and staff. An organization that is equipped to move beyond metrics, mechanics, and minutia can focus on issues of true strategic importance.

Be More Connected to the People in the Organization

Understanding the collective human capital inherent in an organization and connecting with the people who comprise it on a deep and sincere level are important aspects of mastering these new competencies. In many organizations there is a tendency to structure work groups using organizational charts. We see people in boxes, with functions above or below their names. We look at them as parts of the collective whole, but sometimes only from a quantitative standpoint: How many full-time employees do we have? How big is our board? How many people can serve on our committees?

But by structuring work groups using organizational charts, leaders often fail to see their people as individuals, what their hopes and aspirations are, what motivates them, what energizes them, what scares them, and what pleases them. Leaders should ask the fundamental question, "Who is the person in front of me?" and leverage the full human potential within the organization.

Connecting on a deeper level with the individual members and staff comprising an organization maximizes the potential of both. Creating a culture that understands people on a deeper level as individuals serves a strategic advantage, helping to create and sustain positive change.

Ask Powerful Questions

By using open-ended questions, leaders create an environment in which the free exchange of ideas moves the organization forward. Association leaders must recognize that such questions should not be limited to staff and board meetings but that they have application in nearly all situations. Questioning creates an opportunity for coaching within an organization, a culture in which individuals are enabled, empowered, and energized to envision, to work toward, and to achieve their goals.

Association leaders should train their boards to avoid involving themselves with operational details, to maintain a strategic focus and to develop more productive working relationships that can be sustained over time.

Be More Conscious of the World Around You

In our research with all kinds of organizations, we found that the concept of how the organization affects the world around it may be the least understood and least focused on, and yet we believe it is among the most essential. No organization exists in a vacuum. The interconnectedness of our world spurred on by technology in the past 15–20 years—the ability to communicate and conduct commerce across boundaries, borders, and continents—has driven home the point that we are not alone.

Being more aware of the world around you is not necessarily related to global initiatives. The planet can be outside your front door, down your street, in your business center. Or it can be within your industry or profession or in related industries and professions. As a leader, you must recognize your organization's impact on its relative external world; this is an important element in mastering these new leadership competencies.

Start the Conversation

Leaders have a responsibility to initiate the conversation about organizational foundations and leadership competencies in their organizations. An excellent method for doing so is to use the questions for discussion at the end of each chapter in this book. These are not exhaustive, and the answers will be different for every organization. Leaders who are committed to developing greater mastery of the six emerging competencies of leadership, evaluating the existence and relative strength of the eight essential organizational foundations, and embracing the notion of co-creating the future will move their associations forward and model individual leadership behaviors and attributes that will inspire both current and future leaders.

We hope that these conversations will lead to great success for you in creating and sustaining positive change in your organization and for you as a leader in enhancing your ability to think, lead, and achieve!

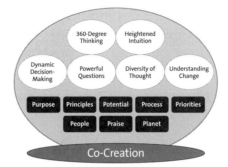

Thoughts to Consider—
An Individual and
Organizational Diagnostic

O N THE FOLLOWING PAGES, we have reproduced all the "thoughts to consider" questions that were included at the end of each chapter, and we hope that you will use them as a diagnostic tool and a dialogue starter in your associations and among your leadership teams. These questions are meant to help you begin to think about the current mastery and applicability of these competencies and foundations both in your organization and in yourself as a leader.

And we hope to keep the conversation going! As you initiate your dialogues, if you identify additional questions that you think would be of value to other leaders, please contact us and share them so we can include them in future editions and communications.

Thoughts to Consider About the
Six Emerging Leadership Competencies

Thoughts to Consider About 360-Degree Thinking

- What kinds of information, am I as an individual leader looking at all the time?
- Do my board members or I fall into tunnel vision?
- How aware am I of peripheral information?
- What are my information filters?
- Do my board and I have the capacity for *connessione?*
- How can I use reflective questions to step back and see patterns in this information and knowledge?
- Are my board and I aware of our individual or collective brain preferences?
- How can 360-degree thinking benefit me as a leader or my board or my organization?

Thoughts to Consider About Heightened Intuition

- What do I know about my own intuition?
- When do I hear it in my thought or decision-making process?
- When I am in the process of decision-making, do I know or listen to how I feel about the issue at hand?
- What do my instincts tell me about the issue at hand?
- How do my instincts affect how I perceive the issue at hand?
- What do I know about my emotional intelligence capacity?
- How can our organization's groups work to develop shared intuition?
- How can we keep our board out of "groupthink" or tunnel vision?
- How can I improve the intuitive mechanisms of my board or my organization?

Thoughts to Consider About Dynamic Decision-Making

- How do I make decisions as a leader today?
- What role does intuition play in my decisions?
- What role does data play?
- How do I balance the need for both?
- How does my association board make decisions today?
- What would the potential be for my organization to integrate intuition in our decision-making process?
- What would be the benefits?
- What would be the risks?

Thoughts to Consider About Powerful Questions

- How do I typically ask questions?
- What questions do I ask? Are they phrased in a positive manner, or are they seeking to place blame?
- What patterns do I see in the answers to the questions I ask?
- How actively do I listen when others speak?
- How well do I prepare for a discussion by reviewing the data about an issue and preparing substantive, powerful questions to be used in group dialogue?
- How does our board structure conversations to be open and engaging? Do we use questions to ensure full discussion and participation?
- Do we support the use of powerful questions and take the time to answer them?
- How and when can I ask one of the most powerful questions of all: "What questions are we most afraid to ask?"
- What can I do to create an organizational culture in which powerful questions are encouraged and appreciated?

Thoughts to Consider About Diversity of Thought
- How does our board engage in diverse dialogue?
- How does our board of directors respond to ideas that are "out of the mainstream"?
- How does our board of directors encourage disagreement in dialogue?
- How do we ensure we examine an issue from multiple perspectives?
- How does our leadership culture appeal to members who have a variety of thinking styles?
- How do we ensure our organization's leadership has diverse perspectives?

Thoughts to Consider About Understanding Change
- What kinds of change have I as an individual leader been asked to lead?
- What do I know about the nature of resistance to those changes?
- What do I understand about helping people and organizations identify the barriers to change?
- How can I gain a better understanding of my own barriers to change?
- What role could coaching play in my organization to help break down the barriers to change?

Thoughts to Consider About the Eight Essential Foundations

Thoughts to Consider About Purpose
- Why does our organization exist?
- In a single sentence, what is our organization's purpose?
- What does purpose mean for our organization's culture?
- What value has our organization always created and what value could we never envision ceasing to create?

- Has our purpose adjusted with changes over time? Has it preserved a uniqueness of focus that gives our organization the courage to change?

- If someone were to look only at our organization's priorities (goals), what would they say our purpose is?

- If we were to ask our committees or other stakeholder groups about our organization's purpose, what would they say it is and why? Would they all say the same thing?

Thoughts to Consider About Principles

- What are our organization's principles? How do we know these are our organization's principles?

- How do our organization's principles guide what we chose to do and chose not to do?

- How do our organization's principles affect how we treat our people?

- How are our organization's principles expressed to others within and outside of the organization?

- If someone were to observe our organization's actions and accomplishments, what would they say our principles are?

- If we were to ask our committees or other stakeholder groups about our organization's principles, what would they say they are and why? Would they all say the same thing?

- Do our principles and practices support change?

- What specific values are essential?

- What behaviors are associated with these values?

Thoughts to Consider About Potential

- Does our organization have an articulated vision statement?

- Does this vision statement clearly define what the organization and its environment would be like if full potential were reached?

- How is our vision for the future linked to our organization's purpose?

- How do our organization's principles influence our vision of the future?

- Is there widespread buy-in of this vision by volunteer and staff leadership?

- Would we know if we had reached our full potential? If we had, would we continue to keep our vision statements or declare success and move on to articulating a new vision?

- What outcomes is our organization able to achieve more effectively because of committing to our potential?

Thoughts to Consider About Process

- What is the role of process in sustaining organizational change? What processes should be in place, and how does our association make them a sustained and positive part of our culture?

- Has our association institutionalized repeatable, effective processes?

- Do we have mechanisms for measuring progress toward our full potential?

- Have we institutionalized strategic and operational planning processes?

- Do those processes allow us to select priorities that move us toward our full potential?

- Are our processes aligned with our purpose and principles, and do we successfully engage and involve people in it?

Thoughts to Consider About Priorities

- Do all our organization's priorities flow from our purpose? If not, which ones do not link to our purpose, and what should we do about that?

- What do we as an organization do well? How do these core competences affect what we chose to do or not to do?

- What do we as an organization not do well? How does this understanding affect what we chose to do or not to do?

- How do organizations that successfully sustain change decide what to focus on? How can our organization mimic their methods?

- What are the cultural implications of deciding not to do something? How do those decisions affect the direction and velocity with which our organization moves toward change?

- What are our resources and what are the existing limitations of those resources? How effectively are we using our resources? How does our understanding of our limited resources affect what we chose to do or not to do?

- Do we routinely evaluate our programs and services to ensure they align with our purpose and create value?

- How do we respond to unanticipated opportunities and threats?

Thoughts to Consider About People

- What are our understandings about the roles that people play in our organization's board, committees, and staff? How do we develop a shared understanding of these roles?

- How do the organization's purpose, practices, and principles affect how people are regarded, how leaders lead, and how members, staff, and customers are treated?

- What are the unique skills, knowledge, and relationships that members bring to the organization?

- What factors allow people to become fully engaged in change?

- Do we clearly communicate to members and staff before the start of a project who is responsible for what and why?

- What should the board do and what should it delegate?

- Is the board of directors empowered to govern the organization?

- Is the chief staff officer empowered to manage the organization?

- Are committees and other stakeholder groups empowered to do the work that they have been delegated, within parameters set by the board?

- How do we ensure that the skills of our members are aligned with the roles in which we ask them to serve?

Thoughts to Consider About Praise

- What role do praise, recognition, and valuing contributions play in our association?
- What are the implications of celebrating success, even if we are still part way along the journey?
- How does our organization express appreciation for member contributions and accomplishments?
- How does our organization express appreciation for staff contributions and accomplishments? Do our methods of rewarding staff reflect what they value as recognition of their contributions?
- How does our organization communicate and celebrate organizational accomplishments?
- What opportunities are there for our organization to achieve external validation through awards, media coverage, government proclamations, and such?
- When we thank individuals for their contributions, do we recognize specific behaviors?

Thoughts to Consider About Planet

- How would the world be different if our organization didn't exist?
- How do we create value for our members and stakeholders?
- How does what we do effect the community outside our organization?
- What are the ripple effects of the programs and services we provide?
- What opportunities that align with our purpose and principles do we have to create positive change not just within our organization but also within the world?

• How does our organization connect with the world around it?

Thoughts to Consider About the Unifying Strategy of Co-Creation: How Leaders Lead Together

• What does it mean to say that co-creation is a partnership between people all across an organization?

• How do we create an atmosphere that encourages the open exchange of ideas?

• How do we express the value of ideas, regardless of who comes up with them?

• How do we foster a shared ownership of organizational goals and outcomes?

• Why is co-creation necessary to create lasting change?

• How do we ensure partnerships where there is truly a shared investment and commitment to success?

• How can we make co-creation a reality? How do we get to the third level of thinking about "us" in balanced partnership together?

Sources and Suggested Reading

1. Adams, Marilee G. *Change Your Questions, Change Your Life: 10 Powerful Tools for Life and Work.* Berrett Kohler. 2004.

2. Alcorn, Shelly, CAE. "Association Executives: Provocative Proposals for Change." Research to be published on corporate website www.alcornassociates.com/index-13.html. 2012.

3. Argyris, Chris. *Knowledge for Action: A Guide to Overcoming Barriers to Organizational Change.* Jossey-Bass. 1993.

4. Adye, Patti. "Intuition and Leadership: The Art of Wise Decision-Making." Master's Thesis for Royal Rods University, Victoria, British Columbia (2004). Retrieved from www.proquest.com. (3177390)

5. Bazerman, M.H. *Judgment in Managerial Decision-Making* (6th ed). Wiley. 2006.

6. Bennis, Warren G. and Thomas, Robert J. *Geeks & Geezers: How Era, Values, and Defining Moments Shape Leaders.* Harvard Business Review Press. 2002.

7. Blanchard, Kenneth H.; Hersey, Paul H.; and Johnson, Dewey E. *Management of Organizational Behavior* (9th ed). Prentice Hall. 2007.

8. Bolman, Lee G. and Deal, Terrence E. *Reframing Organizations: Artistry, Choice, and Leadership* (4th ed). Jossey-Bass. 2008.

9. Bonabeau, Eric. "Don't Trust Your Gut." *Harvard Business Review.* May 2003.

10. Burke, L.A. and Miller, M.K. "Taking the Mystery Out of Intuitive Decision-Making." *Academy of Management Executive,* 13(4), 1999.

11. Church, M.J. "Intuition, Leadership, and Decision-Making: A Phenomenon." 2005. Unpublished dissertation, University of Phoenix. Dissertation Abstracts International, 66(05):1847. (UMI No. 3177390).

12. Coleman, John; Gulati, Daniel; Segovia, W. Oliver. *Passion and Purpose: Stories from the Best and Brightest Young Business Leaders.* Harvard Business Review Press. 2011.

13. Collins, James C. and Porras, Jerry I. *Built to Last: Successful Habits of Visionary Companies.* Harper Collins. 1994.

14. Collins, James C. *Good to Great and the Social Sectors: A Monograph to Accompany Good to Great.* Harper Collins. 2005.

15. Collins, James C. *Good to Great: Why Some Companies Make the Leap...And Others Don't.* Harper Business. 2001.

16. Dalton, James and Dignam, Monica. *The Decision to Join: How Individuals Determine Value and Why They Choose to Belong.* ASAE. 2007.

17. Dalton, James and Dignam, Monica. *10 Lessons for Cultivating Member Commitment: Critical Strategies for Fostering Value, Involvement, and Belonging.* ASAE Association Management Press. 2012.

18. Dane, Erik and Pratt, Michael G. "Exploring Intuition and Its Role in Managerial Decision-Making." *Academy of Management Review,* 32(1), 2007.

19. Drury, M.L. and Kitsopoulos, S.C. "Do You Still Believe in The Seven Deadly Myths?" *Consulting to Management.* March 2005.

20. Epstein, Seymour. "Integration of the Cognitive and the Psychodynamic Unconscious," *American Psychologist,* vol. 49, 1994.

21. Frederick, William C. *Values, Nature, and Culture in the American Organization.* Oxford University Press. 1995.

22. Gelb, Michael. *How to Think Like Leonardo da Vinci: Seven Steps to Genius Every Day.* Dell. 2000.

23. Gladwell, Malcolm. *Blink: The Power of Thinking Without Thinking.* Little, Brown and Co. 2005.

24. Goleman, Daniel. *Leadership: The Power of Emotional Intelligence.* More Than Sound. 2011.

25. Goleman, Daniel; Boyatzis, Richard; and McKee, Annie. *Primal Leadership.* Harvard Business Review Press. 2002.

26. Goleman, Daniel; Boyatzis, Richard; and McKee, Annie. "Primal Leadership: Hidden Drivers of Great Performance." *Harvard Business Review,* December 2001.

27. Goleman, Daniel. *Emotional Intelligence: Why It Can Matter More Than IQ.* Bloomsbury. 1996.

28. Goleman, Daniel. "What Makes A Leader?" *Harvard Business Review.* November-December 1998.

29. Hain, Randy. "The Diversity of Thought." Corporate website article from http://www.belloaks.com/insights/manage-your-career/9/34-diversity-of-thought-the-next-frontier-.

30. Heifetz, Ronald; Grashow, Alexander; and Linsky, Marty. *The Practice of Adaptive Leadership Tools and Tactics for Changing Your Organization and the World.* Harvard Business Press. 2009.

31. Herrmann, Ned. *The Whole Brain Business Book: Unlocking the Power of Whole-Brain Thinking in Organizations and Individuals.* McGraw-Hill. 1996.

32. Hofstede, Geert S. *Cultures and Organizations: Software of the Mind.* McGraw-Hill. 1996.

33. Hofstede, Geert S. "Cultural Constraints in Management." *Academy of Management Executive,* 7(1), 1980.

34. Institute of Leadership & Management. *Creating a Coaching Culture.* www.I-L-M.com/research-and-comment/9617.aspx. May 2011.

35. ITAP International. "Culture in the Workplace Questionnaire." *Certification Training Manual,* 2011. http://www.itapintl.com/tools/culture-in-the-workplace-questionnaire-cw/itapcwquestionnaire.html.

36. Janis, Irving L. *Victims of Groupthink: A Psychological Study of Foreign Policy Decisions and Fiascoes.* Houghton Mifflin. 1972.

37. Jung, Carl. *Psychological Types (The Collected Works of C. G. Jung, Vol. 6).* Princeton University Press. 1976. (Originally published in 1921.)

38. Kahneman, Daniel. *Thinking, Fast and Slow.* Farrar, Straus and Giroux. 2011.

39. Katzenbach, Jon and Smith, Douglas. *The Wisdom of Teams: Creating the High-Performance Organization.* Harper Business. 2003.

40. Kegan, Robert and Lahey, Lisa Laskow. *Immunity to Change: How to Overcome It and Unlock the Potential in Yourself and Your Organization.* Harvard Business School Press. 2009.

41. Keller, Scott and Price, Colin. *Beyond Performance: How Great Organizations Build Ultimate Competitive Advantage.* Wiley. 2011.

42. Klein, Gary. *The Power of Intuition: How to Use Your Gut Feelings to Make Better Decisions at Work.* Crown Business. 2004.

43. Kline, Dee Ann. "Intuitive Team Decision-Making." In *How Professionals Make Decisions.* (Henry Montgomery, Raanan Lipshitz, and Bennett Brehner, eds). Lawrence Erlbaum Associates. 2005.

44. Kotter, John P. *Leading Change.* Harvard Business Review Press. 1996.

45. Kouzes, James M. and Posner, Barry Z. *The Leadesrhip Challenge.* Jossey-Bass. 2007.

46. Lencioni, Patrick. *Overcoming the Five Dysfunctions of a Team: A Field Guide for Leaders, Managers, and Facilitators.* Jossey-Bass. 2005.

47. Linsky, Marty and Heifetz, Ronald. *Leadership on the Line: Staying Alive Through the Dangers of Leading.* Harvard Business Review Press. 2002.

48. Maltbia, Terrence and Power, Anne. *A Leader's Guide to Leveraging Diversity: Strategic Learning Capabilities for Breakthrough Performance.* Butterworth-Heinemann. 2008.

49. Marquardt, Michael J. *Leading with Questions: How Leaders Find the Right Solutions By Knowing What To Ask.* Jossey-Bass. 2005.

50. Mayer, J.D. and Salovey, Peter. "What Is Emotional Intelligence?" In *Emotional Development and Emotional Intelligence: Educational Implications.* (Peter Salovey and David Sluyter, eds). Basic Books. 1997.

51. McNaught, Jay E. "How Baby-Boomer Experienced Leaders Use Intuition in Decision-Making." Dissertation submitted to the Faculty Division of Graduate Studies in Leadership and the Graduate School in partial fulfillment of the requirements for the degree of doctor of education in organizational leadership, Indiana Wesleyan University. April 2012.

52. Miller, C. and Ireland, R. "Intuition in Strategic Decision-Making: Friend or Foe in the Fast-Paced 21st Century?" *Academy of Management Executive,* 19(1), 2005.

53. Moore, James F. *The Death of Competition: Leadership and Strategy in the Age of Business Ecosystems.* Wiley. 1997.

54. Notter, Jamie. "The Power of Frustration." May 4, 2009. http://www.getmejamienotter.com/2009/05/the-power-of-frustration/.

55. Peters, Thomas J. and Waterman, Robert H. Jr. *In Search of Excellence.* Harper & Row. 1982.

56. Quatro, Scott A. and Sims, Ronald R., eds. *Executive Ethics: Ethical Dilemmas and Challenges for the C Suite.* Information Age Publishing. 2008.

57. Rees, Fran. *The Facilitator Excellence Handbook.* Pfeiffer. 1998.

58. Rosenbaum, Steve. *Curation Nation: How to Win in a World Where Consumers Are Creators.* McGraw-Hill. 2011.

59. Sadler-Smith, Eugene and Shefy, Erella. "The Intuitive Executive: Understanding and Applying 'Gut Feel' in Decision-Making." *Academy of Management Executive,* 18(4), 2004.

60. Schein, Edgar H. *Organizational Culture and Leadership.* Jossey-Bass. 2004.

61. Scott, Susan. *Fierce Conversations, Achieving Success at Work and in Life, One Conversation at a Time.* Berkley Trade. 2004.

62. Scott, Susan. *Fierce Leadership: A Bold Alternative to the Worst "Best" Practices of Business Today.* Crown Business. 2011.

63. Senge, Peter M. *The Fifth Discipline: The Art and Practice of the Learning Organization*. Doubleday Business 1994.

64. Shvetank Shah; Horne, Andrew; and Capellá, Jaime. "Good Data Won't Guarantee Good Decisions." *Harvard Business Review*. April 2012.

65. Simon, Herbert A. *Administrative Behaviour: A Study of Decision-Making Processes in Administrative Organizations*. The Free Press. 1997.

66. Simon, Herbert A. *Models of Man: Social and Rational-Mathematical Essays on Rational Human Behavior in a Social Setting*. Wiley. 1957.

67. Simon, Herbert A. "Designing Organizations for an Information-Rich World," in Martin Greenberger. *Computers, Communication, and the Public Interest*. The Johns Hopkins Press. 1971.

68. Stansfield, Brian R, ed. *The Art of Focused Conversation: 100 Ways to Access Group Wisdom in the Workplace*. Canadian Institute of Cultural Affairs. New Society Publishers. 2000.

69. Tecker, Glenn; Frankel, Jean; and Meyer, Paul. *The Will to Govern Well*. ASAE. 2002.

70. Townsend, John. *Leadership Beyond Reason: How Great Leaders Succeed by Harnessing the Power of Their Values, Feelings, and Intuition*. Thomas Nelson. 2009.

71. Traditional Chinese Medicine Basics. Published at website www.tcmbasics.com/basics_5elements.htm.

72. Welch, Jack. *Jack: Straight from the Gut*. Business Plus. 2001.

73. Whitworth, Laura; Kimsey-House, Karen; Kimsey-House, Henry; and Sandahl, Phillip. *Co-Active Coaching: New Skills for Coaching People Toward Success*. Davies-Black. 2007.

74. Williams, Ray B. "The Right-Brained Executive: Use the Right Brain in Business?" *Psychology Today's* Wired for Success Blog. www.psychologytoday.com/blog/wired-success/201006/the-right-brained-executive. June 1, 2010.

75. Winerman, Lea. "What We Know Without Knowing How." *Monitor on Psychology*. (36)(3), 2005.